Praise for Cho

A True Gift

"If you want a better understanding of guitar chords and progressions this is the book to get. This book lays it all out. The construction of triads, 7ths, 9ths, dominant and sus. Guitar head has a special way of teaching. Subject is easy to understand. My first purchase from Guitar head was "Fretboard learning in 24 hours" which was a Godsend. I have since purchased their other books. This book definitely does take away the mystery of chord theory. I HIGHLY recommend this book to anyone looking to enhance their guitar playing knowledge!"

— *Dan & Robin*

More than chords

"I purchased this book for my grandson. This book has so much information about not only chords but various scales and other information my grandson is studying in school."

— *Catherine*

Another Great Guitar Head Book

"An excellent chord instructional that is good for both self-study or to be used by an instructor teaching from beginners who know the basics (NOT good for complete beginners) up through intermediate guitarists. Well worth the price."

— *Arktiem*

Practical Apporach

"Authoritative configuration of chord formation. I liked the theoretical approach, very logical. Good use of total fretboard. I highly recommend."

— *Edwin Poquette*

GUITAR CHORDS BIBLE

INSTANT ACCESS — TO 1053 CHORDS — WITH CHORD — FUNCTIONS AND — PROGRESSIONS

GUITAR HEAD

GH@theguitarhead.com

www.facebook.com/theguitarhead/

Disclaimer

Dedication

We dedicate this book to the complete
Guitar Head team,
supporters, well-wishers and
the Guitar Head community.

It goes without saying that we
would not have gotten
this far without
your encouragement,
critique and support.

Table of Contents

Free Guitar Head Bonuses

Lifetime access to Guitar Head Community

Being around like-minded people is the first step to being successful at anything. The Guitar Head community is a place where you can find people who are willing to listen to your music, answer your questions or talk anything guitar.

Email newsletters sent directly to your inbox

We send regular guitar lessons and tips to all our subscribers. Our subscribers are also the first to know about Guitar Head giveaways and holiday discounts.

Free PDF

Guitar mastery is all about the details! Getting the small things right and avoiding mistakes that can slow your guitar journey by years. So, we wrote a book about 25 of the most common mistakes guitarists make and decided to give it for free to all Guitar Head readers.

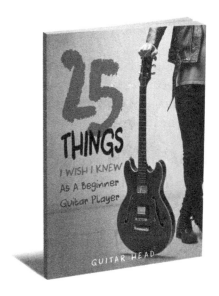

You can grab a copy of the free book and subscribe to newsletter by following the link below.

All these bonuses are a 100% free, with no strings attached. You won't need to enter any personal details other than your first name and email address.

To get your bonuses, go to: ***www.theguitarhead.com/bonus***

Book Profile

Difficulty Level: Intermediate - Advanced

Technical knowledge you need before reading this book:

This book is for guitarists who are familiar with chords theory and its inner mechanisms. Recommended for guitarists looking to learn new and exciting voicings to add flavour to their progressions.

Recommended skills before this book:

- Foundation level introduction to chord formulas

- Strumming and basic concepts of rhythm.

- Knowledge of open, barre chords, triads, and 7th chords.

Note: Advanced guitar tab notation index is included at the end of the book.

Suggested reading before this book:

Chord Theory Demystified: Unlock 531 Beginner Chords Using the CAGED System and Practical Examples.

The first step to writing your own music and creating your own chord progressions is understanding the chemistry of chords.

To understand the chord formulas and how to play the same chord in different places on the fretboard using the CAGED system, I suggest our book Chord Theory Demystified.

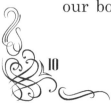

Introduction

You are holding in your hands a gateway of sorts. A tome dedicated to the knowledge of harmony, a vast volume of voicings, a scintillating source of shapes and patterns for the most magical of matrices: the guitar fretboard!

Yes, my friend, you have in your hands a copy of the one and only *Guitar Chords Bible*.

Let that sink in. Sit still for a moment and absorb the magnetism of this compendium. Allow its power to seep in through your fingers, through your hands, and finally into the deep layers of your subconscious mind where it will fuse with the infinite creative spirit inside you to produce the most marvelous music imaginable!

Inside these pages you will find a treasure trove of practical information you can use to expand your knowledge of guitar chords, harmony, and music theory. By the end, you will have experienced the wide worlds of **triads** both closed and spread, the **CAGED system**, **inversions**, **symmetrical chords**, **extensions**, **alterations**, and **quartal harmony**.

The Guitar Chords Bible is designed for the intermediate to advanced guitarist. It's recommended you have some basic knowledge of the guitar and general music theory, such as the musical alphabet, the names of the strings, how to read music notation and/or guitar tablature, and some understanding of chord/scale relationships.

One crucial aspect to accessing the deepest meaning of this book is by understanding a guitar chord diagram. Let's check out an example to just to clarify:

This is an example of a basic chord diagram for an open position C major chord. When we say "open position", we are referring to the open string up to the 3rd fret.

The strings of the guitar are represented vertically, E-A-D-G-B-E from left to right, and the frets are represented horizontally as they appear on the guitar. An 'X' means the string is muted and an open circle means the open string is played as part of the guitar.

So in this C major chord, we mute the low E string, we play the 3rd fret 'C' on the A string, we play the 2nd fret 'E' on the D string, we have the open G string, we play the 1st fret on the 'C' on the B string, and finally we have the open high E string.

All of that make sense?

The 8 Levels in *The Guitar Chords Bible* are progressive, and the information presented in the early Levels is built and expanded upon in the later Levels. However, feel free at any time to skip to the **Chord Dictionary** at the back of the book. There you will find an array of voicings and shapes you can explore at your leisure! Many of them are presented at various points in the Levels.

If you've ever felt envious of your favorite guitar rock stars and their seemingly limitless vocabulary of chords and voicings — then this is the book for you!

Sure, expanding your knowledge of chords requires some memorization and music theory — but once you understand *how* these chords are constructed, you'll soon discover you have the power to explore and create *any* chord you desire.

Unlocking the secrets to chords is one of the greatest ways to not only gain command of the fret board — but also to fully grasp the mechanics and reasonings for how music works the way it does.

Sound exciting? I can't wait either!

LET US BEGIN...

13

LEVEL 1:
Some Fundamentals

Intro:

Are you prepared for a dive into the wonderful world of guitar chords? I know you must be extremely excited to uncover these mysteries. But wait! First we must review a few basic concepts...

In this Level 1 section, we will review the **major scale** and its **intervals**, the concept of a **triad**, how we derive triads from the Major Scale. Finally, we'll touch base with our good old friends, the **seventh chords**. Sound good? Let's begin.

LEVEL 1 KEYWORDS

major scale, intervals, triads, seventh chords, scale degree, semitones, chord qualities, diatonic chord scale, tonic, dominant

---

Major Scale:

Everyone's familiar with the major scale, right? The major scale is a helpful tool once we start talking about these messy and confusing music theories. I like to think of it as the baseline — a simple, consistent, and neutral point from which we can expand.

So, if we take the major scale in the key of C, we find the notes C-D-E-F-G-A-B-C as shown in **Example 1** below:

Example 1: C Major Scale

(All of the examples in this book will be shown in standard musical notation as well as guitar tablature.)

I know, there are a lot of numbers going on here—and you're probably wondering what they all mean.

Each tone of the major scale has a number associated with it called a **scale degree**. Scale degrees are important because they allow us to identify the individual pitches of a scale in terms of their relationship to the other pitches in the scale.

For example, we can see that 'C' is **1**, 'E' is **3**, and 'G' is **5**. From this, we can say that 'E' is the **third** of 'C' and 'G' is the **fifth** of 'C'.

Intervals:

This notation becomes even more important when we discuss **intervals**. Essentially, an interval is the distance between any two pitches.

We have five types of intervals: **major intervals**, **minor intervals**, **perfect intervals**, **diminished intervals**, and **augmented intervals**.

We measure intervals in what we call **semitones**, which are a distance of one pitch from each other.

"Yikes! How will I ever memorize all of this!" Have no fear, we'll take things step by step.

Check out this diagram in **Example 2** showing the intervals of the C major scale:

Example 2: C Major Scale Intervals

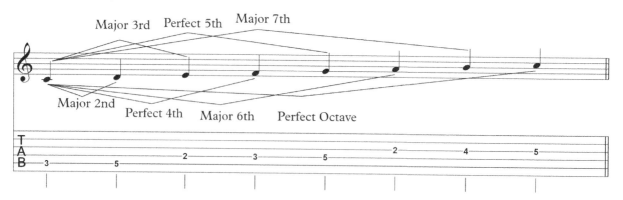

Here's a little math for you: We call the interval from C to D a **major second** because D is *two semitones* away from C.

Remember, we have twelve pitches in our music system: C, C#/Db, D, D#/Eb, E, F, F#/Gb, G, G#/Ab, A, A#/Bb, and B.

C to C# is one semitone, C# to D is one semitone, and 1 + 1 = 2. So we call an interval of two semitones a major second. We call an interval of one semitone a **minor second**.

Using this logic, can you find how many semitones make a **major third**, the distance from C to E? If you said *four semitones*, you got it right! Nice work.

At the risk of scaring you off, here is a chart of all the intervals and their semitone distances — because knowledge is power, right?

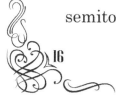

Interval	Semitones
minor second	1
major second	2
minor third	3
major third	4
perfect fourth	5
augment fourth	6
perfect fifth	7
minor sixth	8
major sixth	9
minor seventh	10
major seventh	11
octave	12

Some Exercises:

OK, enough of this theory!

Here are two example exercises to try. First, in **Example 3**, we play the intervals of the C major scale melodically. Oh yeah, I should probably mention...

There are two ways of playing intervals:

1) **Melodically**: one note after another.

2) **Harmonically**: both notes at the same time.

So, here in **Example 3** we play the intervals of the C major scale melodically:

Example 3: C Major Scale Intervals Played Melodically

And here in **Example 4** we play the intervals of the C major scale harmonically:

Example 4: C Major Scale Intervals Played Harmonically

Practice both of these exercises until you feel comfortable with the movements and the sounds of each of these intervals.

Get creative! I'm sure you can find some other places to play them besides where they're notated in the tablature!

Triads:

Now that we've laid the foundation with the major scale, let's begin to learn about **triads** and their qualities and construction.

A triad is simply a group of three notes. Think triangle or triforce — the prefix *tri* signifies a group of three.

For our purposes right now, we have three distinct chord qualities (i.e., sounds) of triads: **major triads**, **minor triads**, and **diminished triads**.

(Later on in Level 7 we'll discuss quartal harmony and learn about some other qualities of triads—but for now let's stick with these three. Baby steps!)

In **Example 5**, we construct the first major triad from the notes of the major scale:

Example 5: Construction of Triad in C Major Scale

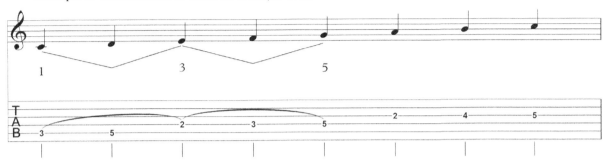

This triad is built from the **first**, **third**, and **fifth** scale degrees. In short, we skip every other tone in the scale to build the first triads.

We can do the same thing starting from D (D-F-A), from E (E-G-B), from F (F-A-C), etc. all the way to B (B-D-F). This gives us what we call a **diatonic chord scale**, which we'll cover in just a moment.

First, let's dive a little deeper into the intervals of these first three triads.

The **major triad** is built from two intervals: a **major third** (or four semitones), followed by a **minor third** (or three semitones). Take a look at **Example 6a**:

Example 6a: Intervals of Major Triad

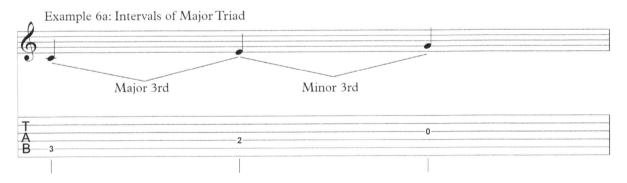

You might recognize this as part of an open position C major chord—but it might be possible you've never thought about it as only three notes like this!

If a handy formula helps you to remember, the major triad is: **1-3-5**.

The second quality we'll discuss is the **minor triad**. To build the minor triad, we make one small adjustment to the major triad: we *flatten* (or lower) the third degree by one semitone.

Take a look at **Example 6b** and compare the intervals of a minor triad with those of a major triad:

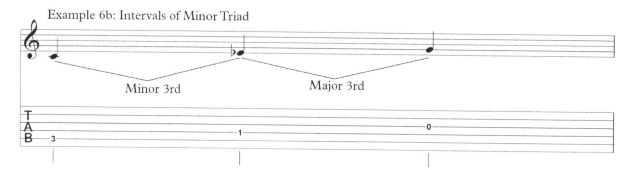

Example 6b: Intervals of Minor Triad

Can you tell me the difference? The intervals are reversed—how strange!

The minor triad begins with a **minor third** (or three semitones), followed by a **major third** (or four semitones).

Music is full of these sorts of interesting symmetries and reflections. One benefit of studying music theory is experiencing a revelation of this balanced beauty found in the sounds, colors and shapes all around you! But I digress...

The formula for a minor triad is **1-b3-5**.

Finally, we reach the third triad quality (for now): the enigmatic **diminished triad**. The diminished triad appears only once in the major scale, on the seventh and final scale degree before we return to our home base of scale degree one.

We'll dive deeper into the diminished triad and its related sounds in Level 4, so for now let's just check out **Example 6c** to learn the intervals of the diminished triad:

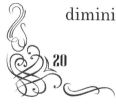

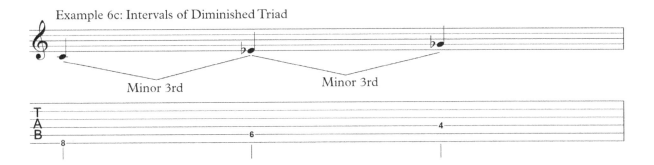

Example 6c: Intervals of Diminished Triad

Minor 3rd

Minor 3rd

Spooky, right? Notice what we did there? We flattened *both* the intervals! So a diminished triad is built from two minor thirds.

The formula for a diminished triad is **1-b3-b5**.

Alright, how are you doing so far? Need a breather from this theory? Me too.

Take a moment to get creative with these three triads. Pick through them, strum them, let your ears soak their sounds.

Go ahead and visit the Chord Dictionary to find other places to play them. See if you can use them to compose a chord progression for yourself. The more time you spend absorbing these sounds, the more effective you will be as an expressive musician!

What is a Diatonic Chord Scale?

Feeling refreshed? Nice work, let's dive back in.

I'd like to revisit something we briefly touched upon previously: how we can use these triads to build a diatonic chord scale.

A diatonic chord scale is simply a collection of all the pitches in a scale played as chords. We can see here in **Example 7** a C major diatonic chord scale:

Example 7: Construction of Diatonic Triads in C Major

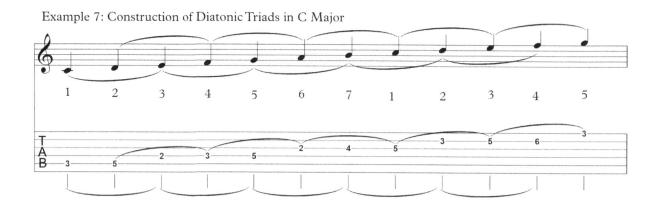

We have seven chords in the C major diatonic chord scale: **C major** (C-E-G), **D minor** (D-F-A), **E minor** (E-G-B), **F major** (F-A-C), **G major** (G-B-D), **A minor** (A-C-E), and **B diminished** (B-D-F).

Try playing them melodically, as in **Example 8**:

Example 8: Diatonic Triads in C Major Played Melodically

Now try them harmonically in two directions. First, horizontally up the neck:

Example 9: Diatonic Triads in C Major Played Harmonically Horizontally up the neck

And second, vertically up the neck:

Example 10: Diatonic Triads in C Major Played Harmonically Vertically up the neck

Great work so far! Remember to look through the Chord Dictionary and see if you can play the diatonic chord scale in C major using some of the other triad shapes listed there.

If you're feeling super ambitious, try to change keys to G or D—or even something more remote if you're *truly* daring, like Ab or Eb!

Like I said before, the more you absorb these sounds and become comfortable with their locations on the guitar fretboard, the more you will grow as a creative, expressive musician!

Seventh Chords:

Now that we've reviewed some of our basic triads, let's add another element to this wacky world of harmony.

What do you know about **seventh chords**? Do they scare you? Do you feel intimidated when you see a G7 or Cmin7b5 on a chord sheet? Do you know some reliable voicings for these chords?

Honestly, these harmonies aren't something to be afraid of or shy away from! These chords add a deeper color to our triads and provide some new and interesting shapes for our fingers to grasp. Let's check 'em out!

In its simplest sense, a seventh chord adds one note to the triad — the **seventh** scale degree. We can see this visually here in **Example 11**:

Example 11: Construction of Diatonic 7th Chords in C Major Scale

In the construction of the major triad, we skipped every other tone in the scale to make the formula 1-3-5, right? So all we do to create the seventh chord is skip one more note to make the formula **1-3-5-7**, or in this example above, C-E-G-B.

We call this a **major seventh** chord. Any questions?

Well, I have some questions for *you*: Do you know the other basic seventh chords? Do you know what transformations we make to the major seventh chord in Example 11 to reach the other qualities of seventh chords?

If yes, then—*woah!*—you are ahead of the game! If not, let's take a closer look together:

In Example 11 we built the major seventh chord. Here are the intervals of the major seventh chord:

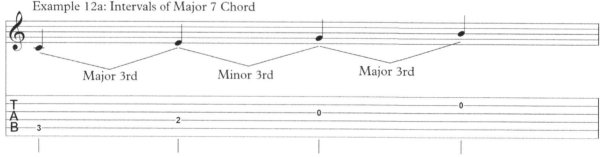

Example 12a: Intervals of Major 7 Chord

Major 3rd   Minor 3rd   Major 3rd

We can see in **Example 12a** above that the major seventh chord is built from a **major third**, followed by a **minor third**, followed by another **major third**. We can also think of it as a major triad with an added major third.

The next quality of seventh chord is the **minor seventh** chord as shown in **Example 12b**:

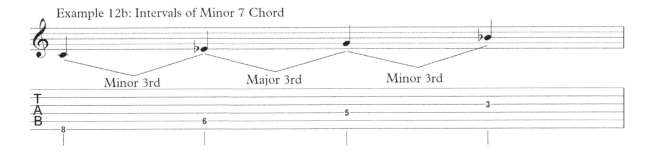

Example 12b: Intervals of Minor 7 Chord

What transformations did we make to the major seventh chord to reach the minor seventh chord? If you said we flatten the third and flatten the seventh, then you are... *checks notes*... absolutely correct!

The formula for a minor seventh chord is **1-b3-5-b7**. In this case it'd be C-Eb-G-Bb. Or we can think of it as a **minor triad** with an added **minor third**.

Hopefully you're not feeling too overwhelmed by this, because we have two more qualities to cover!

Next up, we meet the mighty **dominant seventh** chord. Why do we call it the dominant seventh chord? Good question! Is it because it's so overpowering in any situation that it dominates the sound? Sometimes, yes!

The real answer, however, is a little more complicated. Remember that each tone of the major scale has a number associated with it? So in addition to that, each tone also has another name besides its pitch (C, D, E, etc).

We call the *first degree* of the major scale the **tonic**. Tonic is derived from the Greek word for tone.

We call the *fifth degree* of the major scale **dominant**. In our major scale, this seventh chord first appears on the fifth degree, thus the name dominant seventh.

All the other pitches have these special names too, and we'll continue this discussion later.

Let's look at the intervals of the dominant seventh chord:

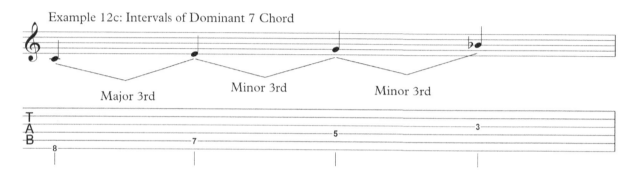

Example 12c: Intervals of Dominant 7 Chord

What transformations did we make to the major seventh chord to reach this dominant seventh chord? If you said we flatten the seventh degree, nice job!

The formula for this dominant seventh chord is **1-3-5-b7**, or in this case C-E-G-Bb. We can also think of it as a **major triad** with a **minor third** added.

The last quality we'll discuss right now is the **minor seventh flat five** chord (or Min7b5). Looks intimidating, but hopefully it's not so bad once you understand what we're doing:

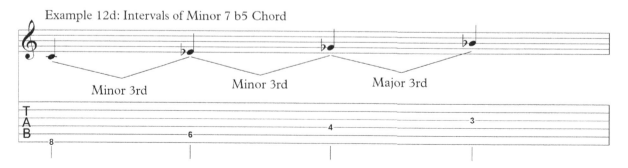

Example 12d: Intervals of Minor 7 b5 Chord

As you can probably tell from its name, this chord can be thought of as a minor seventh chord with a flat fifth degree.

The formula for this chord is **1-b3-b5-b7**, or in this case, C-Eb-Gb-Bb.

This chord begins with a **minor third**, followed by another **minor third**, and ends with a **major third**.

This chord is also sometimes called a **half-diminished** chord because it has a **diminished triad** (C-Eb-Gb) followed by a **major third** (Gb).

A fully **diminished seventh** chord has three minor thirds, but we'll discuss that further in Level 4.

Some Voicings:

I can tell you've had enough theory for the moment. Here, let's take a look at some different voicings for these chords, starting with **Example 13**.

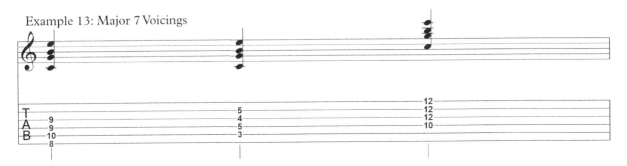

Example 13: Major 7 Voicings

We have notated here the same voicing (C-G-B-E) in three different locations, starting on the low E string, from the A string, and finally from the D string.

We'll discuss inversions of these and other chords in Level 3—so hang tight! Practice memorizing where the root of these chords is and see if you can play them in all twelve keys!

Let's follow the same path as we did earlier. Here are some minor seventh voicings:

Example 14: Minor 7 Voicings

As you recall, to make a major seventh chord into a minor seventh, we flatten the third and seventh degrees. All we've done here is taken the same voicings from our major seventh chord and used those transformations. So we've changed our voicing from C-G-B-E to C-G-Bb-Eb.

Follow me? Hopefully, some visualization of this on the fretboard helps you absorb the theory!

Next, let's try some dominant seventh voicings. Remember, to make the dominant seventh chord, all we do is flatten the seventh degree of our major seventh chord.

Check this out visually in **Example 15**:

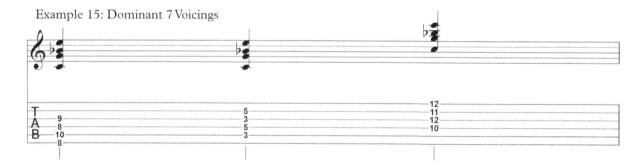

Example 15: Dominant 7 Voicings

We're using the same basic voicing as in the major seventh and minor seventh, just this time we spell it C-G-Bb-E to make C dominant seventh. Neat, huh?

OK, one more group of voicings for you. Let's turn this into a **minor seventh flat five** chord. Remember, all we do is flatten the third, fifth, and seventh scale degrees. Check it out visually in **Example 16** below:

Example 16: Minor 7 b5 Voicings

Are you starting to see some connections between these different chord qualities and how they all build upon one another? I like to think of them as analogous to a color wheel; some chords have darker shades and some have lighter shades. Some voicings feel more open and spacious while others feel denser and more closed.

Just as certain colors complement each other or may look discordant when side-by-side, so too do the tones of music. Once you really get to understanding intervals and chords, you'll realize how the relationship of notes creates certain feelings and moods. Pretty incredible!

Some Example Chord Progressions:

Major, Minor & Diminished Triads and Minor and Dominant Seventh Chords

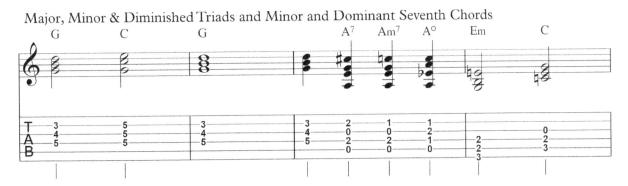

29

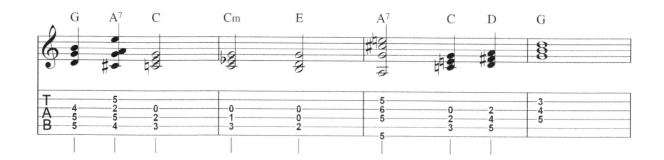

Major, Minor, and Dominant Sevenths in a ii-V-I cycle

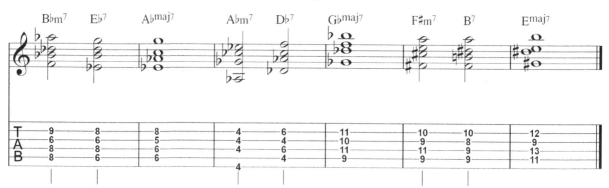

Major and Minor Triads

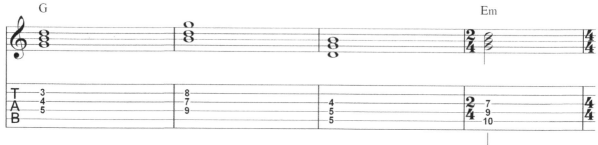

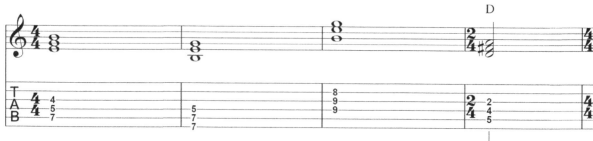

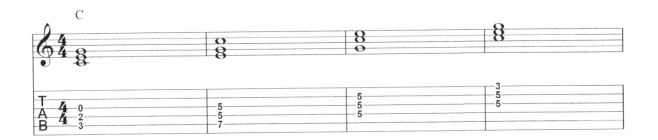

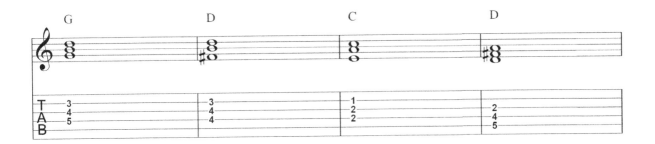

Minor and Dominant Seventh Chords on a Jazz Blues

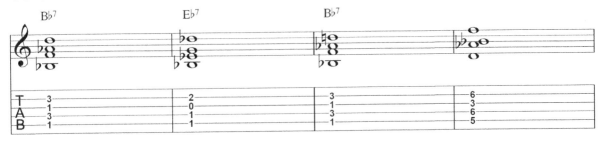

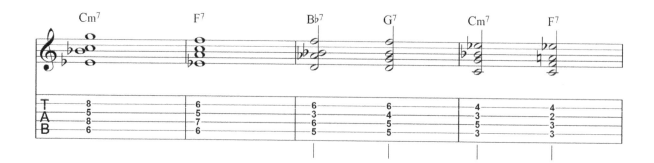

In Conclusion:

It's important for you as a guitarist to create these associations for yourself; once again, the more you absorb and build relationships with all of these sounds, the more effective a musician you will become!

LEVEL 2:
CAGED System

Intro:

Well, look at you! You surpassed the challenges of Level 1. Nice work!

Now that you've been reacquainted with the foundations of the major scale and some basic triads and seventh chords, let us now plunge into the depths of the **CAGED system** and **barre chords**.

Maybe you've heard of barre chords before. Maybe you even know how to play a few. Or maybe you thought barre chords were spelled "bar" chords. I regret to inform you this is not a bar—but maybe, if you practice enough, you can play some of these chords at your next gig at the local bar!

Joking aside, how would you like a cohesive system to memorize and play multiple different qualities of barre chords in every key and in every position on the guitar? This is where the CAGED system becomes extremely useful for guitarists.

> **LEVEL 2 KEYWORDS:**
>
> *CAGED System, barre chords, chord tones*

The CAGED System:

You know by now the five open position chords of C, A, G, E, and D, right? These chords form the basis of what we guitarists call the CAGED system. It is an efficient and easy method for learning and memorizing *hundreds* of different chords!

Like other stringed instruments, with the guitar we can take one chord shape and move it horizontally up the neck to make the same quality of chord in all twelve keys.

Here, let's start at the beginning:

Major Chords:

First take a look at how we move the open positions chords into barre chords. Remember, a barre chord just means that there are elements of our fingering that include playing two or more notes together with one finger.

You can see here in **Example 1** a C major chord played first in open position and second as a barre chord one octave higher:

Example 1: C Major Open Position & Barre Chord Octave Higher

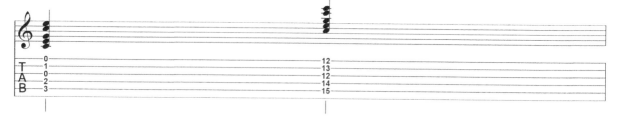

Notice here that we have replaced the open G and E strings in the open position C major chord to the 12th fret notes G and E that we play by barring the 12th fret with our index finger.

It's important to observe that we have the root of this chord on the A string. You'll want to memorize this position, as you might get lost once we start moving these chord shapes around the fretboard.

Let's continue through the rest of the open position chords.

In **Example 2**, we find the same arrangement with an open position A major chord and its barre chord version one octave higher:

Example 2: A Major Open Position & Barre Chord Octave Higher

Again, recognize here that the open low E, A, and high E strings have been replaced by a barre on the 12th fret with our index finger. Please note here the root of this chord is also on the A string.

In **Example 3**, we find the open G chord with its equivalent one octave higher:

Example 3: G Major Open Position & Barre Chord Octave Higher

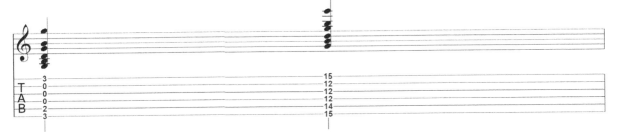

This is one chord you may not be familiar with as a barre chord, but it's extremely useful to have it under your fingers! Notice again which open strings have been replaced by a barre, and also that here the root of the chord is on the low E string.

I trust you know the names of the notes on the low E, A, and D strings, right? If not, I suggest taking some time to familiarize yourself with them; your journey as a guitar player will be much easier as a result.

Continuing on here, let's take a look at **Example 4** — the open E major chord and its equivalent barre chord one octave higher:

Example 4: E Major Open Position & Barre Chord Octave Higher

I'm sure you're already familiar with this chord, since it's often the first barre chord that beginning guitarists will learn. Notice again, the root is on the low E string—and we've replaced the open low E, B, and high E strings with a barre on the 12th fret with our index finger.

One more! (For now...)

In **Example 5**, we see the open position D major chord and a D major barre chord one octave higher:

Example 5: D Major Open Position & Barre Chord Octave Higher

The root of the chord is on the D string, but the spacing can be somewhat more challenging for the beginning guitarist. Make sure to keep one fret distance on the barre chord between the 12th and 14th frets! Otherwise

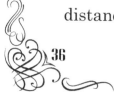

you are liable to play something other than D major (which could be cool, but maybe not what you're intending to do.)

Great work! Now take a break and get creative with the chords:

First, practice moving from the open position to the barre chord.

Next, practice moving the barre chords around while maintaining the proper spacing. Practice strumming them and picking through them to make sure all the notes are sounding properly.

Finally, use the chords to compose some original progressions for yourself.

Minor Chords:

Welcome back! Let's now take a look at how we transform the major barre chords previously discussed into minor barre chords.

Remember from Level 1, the formula for a major triad is **1-3-5** and the formula for a minor triad is **1-b3-5**.

Triads were easier to see the transformations because we only had three notes to look at. In these barre chords, however, we have more than three notes, which means that some **chord tones** will be doubled.

So, let's take a look at our first chord, C minor.

In **Example 6**, we see a C minor chord played here in open position and then as a barre chord one octave higher:

Example 6: C Minor Open Position & Barre Chord Octave Higher

What differences do you see between these two chords here and the C major chords from Example 1? Two important points are the third has been lowered from E to E flat and we have removed the open high E string.

In **Example 7**, let's take a look at A minor as an open position chord and then a barre chord one octave higher:

Example 7: A Minor Open Position & Barre Chord Octave Higher

You may already know this barre chord, as it's a common one for beginners to learn. Notice again the differences between these chords and the A major chords in Example 2. Here the third has been lowered from C sharp in Example 2 to C natural in Example 7.

Continuing on, we find an open position G minor chord and its equivalent barre chord one octave higher in **Example 8**:

Example 8: G Minor Open Position & Barre Chord Octave Higher

We have again flattened the third chord tone, from B natural in Example 3, to B flat in Example 8. We have also removed the high G on the third fret of the high E string to make the chord slightly easier to play. This chord is somewhat obscure, but it's useful to have in your bag of tricks!

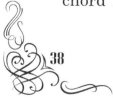

In **Example 9**, we see an E minor chord in open position followed by the same E minor chord one octave higher as a barre chord:

Example 9: E Minor Open Position & Barre Chord Octave Higher

Another common barre chord guitarists learn first. Notice here, the third chord tone in Example 4 (G sharp) has been lowered to G natural, the open G string.

Quick, can you name all the chord tones in this open E minor chord? One ... Two ... Three ... Stop!

Here ya go: the low E string is the root, the second fret on the A string (B) is the fifth, the second fret on the D string (E) is the root, the open G string (G) is the flat third, the open B string (B) is the fifth, and the high E string (E) is again the root.

In this chord voicing we have the root played three times, the fifth played twice, and the third played only once. Stash that in your memory bank; we'll talk more about this later...

Nice work! One final example before we begin linking all this together:

In **Example 10**, we find the open position D minor chord followed by a D minor barre chord one octave higher:

Example 10: D Minor Open Position & Barre Chord Octave Higher

Notice again how we've transformed the D major chord in Example 5 to make this D minor chord in Example 10. The third chord tone has been flattened, meaning in Example 5, we had F sharp as the highest note in the chord — and in Example 10, we have F natural.

As before, make sure you have the proper spacing with this chord, as it can be easy to let your fingers slip!

Before proceeding, I'd like you to now take a moment and play through all of these ten chords.

Shift between the major and minor variations and the barre chords. See if you can comfortably move all the different chords around the fretboard. Pick through them, strum them, try to sing the different tones, try to identify the chord tones (**1-3-5** or **1-b3-5**) of each different voicing.

Piecing It All Together:

Major Shapes

Ready to take everything to the next level? Let's piece together how we can use these five different chord shapes in a connected way to open up many different chord voicings. This is the basis of what we call the CAGED system.

Let's quickly jump back to the beginning. We'll start again with **Example 1**, a basic C major chord in open position:

Example 1: C Major Open Position & Barre Chord Octave Higher

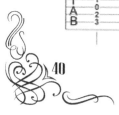

40

Remember the root of this chord is on the A string. Let's label this chord as "**C**" shape.

As I mentioned previously, we can move this shape around the fretboard using the barre chord—and the root always remains on the A string.

So for instance, the same chord shape played two frets higher would be called D major using a "**C**" shape. Follow me?

OK, take a look at this:

Example 11a: C Major Chord Using "A" Shape

In **Example 11a**, we find a C major chord using an "**A**" shape. Remember the open A chord and barre chord we made in Example 2? Here we've taken that chord and made it into C major. Like our "**C**" shape, the root of the "**A**" shape chord is also on the A string. Can you see the connection between these two chord voicings?

The next step:

Example 11b: C Major Chord Using "G" Shape

In **Example 11b**, we play a C major chord using the "**G**" shape. We shifted the G major barre chord we learned in Example 3 into a C major chord.

Do you see how this transformation worked and how this voicing fits in with the other two so far? The root of this chord is on the low E string.

Continuing on, we find in **Example 11c** a C major chord played using the "**E**" shape — or a transformation of the E major barre chord from Example 4:

Example 11c: C Major Using "E" Shape

Like the "**G**" shape, this chord has its root on the low E string. This is likely a common chord for you, but do you see (or rather, hear) how it fits in with the other voicings so far?

Finally, in **Example 11d**, we learn C major played using the "**D**" shape:

Example 11d: C Major Using "D" Shape

The root of this chord is on the D string. The pattern concludes with the second chord in Example 1, the C major barre chord played using the "**C**" shape.

Phew! What a challenge! Are you understanding how all these chord shapes fit together inside of this system? Pretty elegant, don't you think?

42

For complete reference, here is a map of the C-A-G-E-D sequence and voicings on the guitar fretboard:

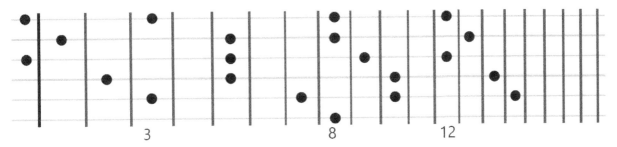

Minor Shapes:

Now that we've connected all the dots with the major shapes, let us turn to the minor shapes and follow the same pathway.

We start back in Example 6, where we learned C minor in open position and as a barre chord one octave higher. This is again our "C" shape—and it's important to remember the transformations we made to get this minor chord from our major chord, as we will follow the same steps with the other four shapes.

Now let's examine **Example 12a**:

Example 12a: C Minor Using "A" Shape

Here we can see a C minor chord played using the "A" shape.

Notice the difference between this C minor chord and the C major chord using the "A" shape we learned previously. Can you see the connection between this voicing and the open position C minor "C" shape?

It's the same idea as the major shapes, just with the third chord tone flattened by one half step!

Next we find a C minor chord played using a "**G**" shape in **Example 12b**:

Example 12b: C Minor Using "G" Shape

Like all the examples of the "**G**" shape, the root of this chord is found on the low E string. We have also adjusted this voicing slightly and replaced the 'E' on the fifth fret of the B string in Example 11b with a 'G' on the 8th fret, as reaching down to an E flat on the B string would be a rather large stretch!

Next, we make a C minor chord using the "**E**" shape:

Example 12c: C Minor Using "E" Shape

See how this chord relates to the E minor barre chord we learned in Example 9? Once again, the root of this chord is on the low E string.

Are you seeing the connection between these different shapes and how they link together? Keep up the good work!

Our final minor shape (for now) is a C minor chord using the "**D**" shape:

Example 12d: C Minor Using "D" Shape

How many times is each chord tone repeated in the chord? One ... Two ... Stop! Heh heh, OK that was a little too quick—but I hope you're getting faster at learning to identify these things!

In this voicing, we have the fifth on the A string, the root on the D string, the fifth on the G string, the root on the B string, and the flat third on the high E string.

Again, the third chord tone is played only once, while the root and fifth are doubled. This is because the third (and the seventh) is what determines the quality of the chord.

If you look at the formula for major chord and minor chords, the only difference comes from the third. Usually it sounds best to only include this voice one time in the chord voicing; the other tones act more as stabilizers, giving weight and depth to the chord, while the third acts more as a flavor. Not a hard and fast rule, of course—but it's good to know why things are the way they are.

You have permission to experiment! Try to alter these chord voicings to include more of third and see how it sounds to you!

Here for reference are all of minor CAGED voicings mapped out on the:

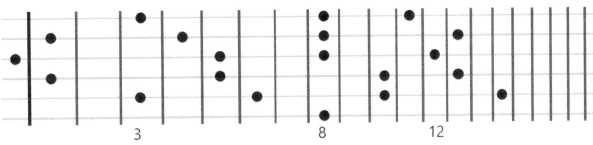

Major 7 Shapes:

Let's explore these sonic depths even further. Now that we've covered the major and minor CAGED shapes, are you ready to construct some different voicings for major seventh, minor seventh, dominant seventh, and minor seventh flat five chords? Only one way to find out!

I trust you remember the formula for a major seventh chord from Level 1: **1-3-5-7**. Skipping every other tone up the scale in C makes C-E-G-B.

How can we transform our "**C**" shape in open position to create a C major seventh?

Example 13a has the answer:

Example 13a: C Major 7 Using "C" Shape

Do you see the difference? We made *one change*, which was lowering the 'C' on the first fret of the B string to a 'B' by simply playing the open string. Pretty simple, huh?

Let's build the same road as we did the major and minor shapes, now with the major seventh shapes.

In **Example 13b**, we find C major seventh played using an "**A**" shape:

Example 13b: C Major 7 Using "A" Shape

Once again, we made one small transformation to this chord. Can you find it?

We moved the 'C' on the third fret of the G string down one half step to 'B'. Not too complex. Like all the other "**A**" shapes, this chord has the root on the A string.

I trust by now you see clearly how this chord fits with the "**C**" shape chord, and you could probably figure out the rest of the major seventh voicings. But just to be thorough, we'll cover them here.

Take a look at C major seventh played using a "**G**" shape in **Example 13c**:

Example 13c: C Major 7 Using "G" Shape

This is a beautiful chord voicing! Pay particular attention to the half step (or minor second) interval between 'B' and 'C'. Tense!

This chord has more transformations compared to the previous two. Notice we shifted our fingering slightly; we now play the 9th fret on the D string with our 4th finger instead of barring the entire 5th fret with our 1st finger, as we did in the major "G" shape.

In **Example 13d**, we learn C major seventh played as an "**E**" shape:

Example 13d: C Major 7 Using "E" Shape

Like the "**C**" and "**A**" shape voicings, we only make one transformation to this chord. We lowered the 'C' on the 10th fret of the D string to a 'B' on the 9th fret. Simple!

This chord has the root and fifth doubled and the third and seventh played once each. Can you identify those voices in this chord?

Finally, in **Example 13e**, we make C major seventh using the "**D**" shape:

Example 13e: C Major 7 Using "D" Shape

You might actually find this chord easier to play than the plain major version of the "**D**" shape.

We have removed the lowest voice in this chord and also lowered the 'C' that was on the 13th fret of the B string to a 'B' on the 12th fret. Easy! Elegant! Beautiful!

Here for your reference is a map of all the major seventh voicings and how they link together:

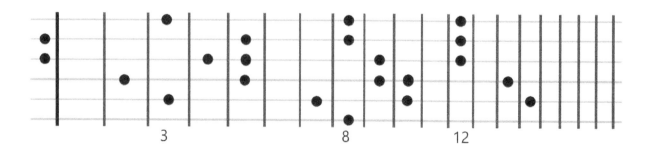

Minor 7 Shapes:

We will now turn to the CAGED minor seventh shapes. Remember from Level 1, the formula for minor seventh is **1-b3-5-b7**; so in the key of C, that means C-Eb-G-Bb.

Let's take a look at how we turn the open position "**C**" shape into a minor seventh voicing. We can see this in **Example 14a**:

Example 14a: C Minor 7 Using "C" Shape

How does this chord shape differ from the minor "**C**" shape from Example 6? In this example, we replaced the "G" played by the open G string to a "Bb" played on the 3rd fret of the G string.

Here is a perfect example of voice substitution. I said earlier that the third and seventh are the tones that define the quality of any chord. So, if we want to play a seventh chord (and don't have a convenient place for it in our original voicing) we can swap out either the fifth or the root for the seventh. Make sense?

Next, let's look at C minor seventh played at an "**A**" shape:

Example 14b: C Minor 7 Using "A" Shape

What differences can you find between this chord and the original "**A**" shape minor voicing we learned previously? In this chord, we lowered the

'C' on the 5th fret of the G string down to a 'Bb' on the 3rd fret of the G string.

Practice jumping back and forth between these two voicings and see if you can hear a difference in the color of the chords. Is one darker or lighter than the other? Is one more or less dense than the other? What is the difference in mood between these two chords?

In **Example 14c**, we see the C minor seventh played as a "G" shape chord:

Example 14c: C Minor 7 Using "G" Shape

This chord bears more resemblance to the "G" shape major seventh than the "G" shape minor voicing, in my opinion. Again, in this chord, we have shifted the fingering away from the barre on the 5th fret, to play the 8th fret on the D string with our 4th finger.

Notice also, this chord voicing has the same notes and spacing as the "C" shape in Example 14a. To master the fretboard, it's important to notice these sorts of patterns on the guitar!

In contrast, the "E" shape C minor seventh is a super barre chord. Take a look at it here in **Example 14d**:

Example 14d: C Minor 7 Using "E" Shape

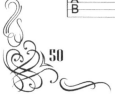

In this chord, we barre the entire 8th fret with our 1st finger and then add the 10th fret on the A string with our 3rd finger. Like the other "**E**" shape chords, the root is found on the low E string.

Lastly, let's look at C minor seventh played as a "**D**" shape chord.

Example 14e: C Minor 7 Using "D" Shape

This chord resembles the "**D**" shape major seventh in that it only contains 4 notes — each of the chord tones played once. How simple! Like the other "**D**" shapes, this one has its root on the D string.

I hope you are able to see the transformations between this chord, the original "**D**" shape minor voicing, and the major voicings we have learned so far.

Again, for your reference, here is a map of all the minor seventh voicings on the fretboard:

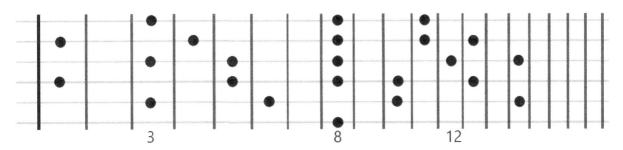

Dominant 7 Shapes:

Next, let's turn to the dominant seventh CAGED voicings. Remember the formula for the dominant seventh chord is **1-3-5-b7**—or in the key of C, C-E-G-Bb.

To turn the open position "**C**" shape into a dominant seventh chord, all we need to do is add 'Bb'.

Can you figure this out without the visual?

Here, see if you were right:

Example 15a: C Dominant 7 Using "C" Shape

Notice in this chord, we have replaced the 'G' played by the open G string with 'Bb' on the 3rd fret of the G string. Also, similar to the "**C**" shape minor seventh voicing, we have replaced the fifth scale degree with the seventh.

Here's a question: Can you take this chord voicing and turn it into C dominant nine? Think about it... we'll talk more about that later...

In **Example 15b**, we visit C dominant seventh as an "**A**" shape:

Example 15b: C Dominant 7 Using "A" Shape

We have replaced the 'C' on the 5th fret of the G string with 'Bb' played on the 3rd fret of the G string. Like the other "**A**" shapes, the root of this chord is found on the A string.

Example 15c: C Dominant 7 Using "G" Shape

In **Example 15c** above, we can see C dominant seventh played as a "**G**" shape chord. Like the "**G**" shape minor seventh voicing, this voicing has the same order and spacing of pitches as the "**C**" shape chord—only it's played from the 8th fret of the low E string. See the connection?

Take a look at the "**E**" shape dominant seventh chord in **Example 15d**:

Example 15d: C Dominant 7 Using "E" Shape

You may know this chord already; if so, hopefully now you see how this chord connects with all the other CAGED voicings.

Finally, let's look at the "**D**" shape dominant seventh voicing here in **Example 15e**:

Example 15e: C Dominant 7 Using "D" Shape

Like the other "**D**" shape seventh chords, this one contains only four tones, each of the chord tones played once. Very simple and clean sound.

Here again is the map of all the CAGED dominant seventh voicings on the fretboard:

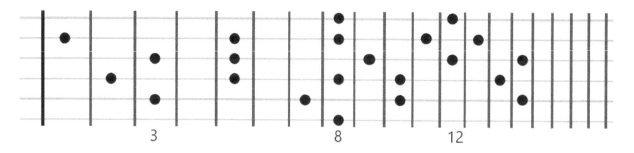

Minor 7 b5 Shape:

So how ya feeling? Brain a little fried?

I hope this isn't too overwhelming for you. On a positive note, I bet you're starting to see how all these different chord voicings are connected, and you're developing an ability to move freely between them! Pretty soon you're going to be a fully-fledged rock star!

We have one more quality to move through the CAGED system: the minor seventh flat five chords.

Remember the formula for minor seventh flat five is **1-b3-b5-b7**—or in the key of C, we spell it C-Eb-Gb-Bb.

Let's take a look at how we move this quality through the CAGED system.

In **Example 16a**, we will look at C minor seventh flat five played as a "C" shape:

Example 16a: C Minor 7 b5 Using "C" Shape

What similarities do you see between this chord and the "**C**" shape minor seventh chord? Basically, all we've done here is add 'Gb' to the top of the chord on the 2nd fret of the high E string. Not too complex, right?

In this chord, it's important that we include the fifth scale degree. Minor seventh flat five is one exception to the rule of substituting voices we have been discussing. The only difference between the minor seventh and this one is the flat five scale degree, so it's imperative we include it to get the true color of the chord.

Moving on, we can see C minor seventh flat five played as an "**A**" shape chord in **Example 16b**:

Example 16b: C Minor 7 b5 Using "A" Shape

Notice here, we only have 4 voices in this chord: the **root**, the **flat five**, the **flat seventh**, and the **flat third**. Each voice is played only one time.

Like the other "**A**" shape chords, the root is found on the A string. This is a versatile chord, and we'll talk about some other applications of it later on.

Here's the "**G**" shape of C minor seventh flat five in **Example 16c**:

Example 16c: C Minor 7 b5 Using "G" Shape

This chord shape is the most drastically different of any of the other voicings so far. We abandon the barre from the major chords and the notes on the D string from the dominant and minor seventh voicings in favor of only four voices in the order of **root**, **flat seventh**, **flat third**, and **flat fifth**.

In **Example 16d**, we see C minor seventh flat five played as an "E" shape chord:

Example 16d: C Minor 7 b5 Using "E" Shape

This is the minor seventh flat five chord with the most voices. Can you identify which voices are doubled in this shape?

We have the root on the E string, the flat five on the A string, the flat seventh on the D string, the flat third on the G string, the flat seventh on the B string, and finally the root again on the high E string.

See how we still only have the third scale degree voiced one time in the chord, while the root, fifth, and seventh are doubled? Those thirds have got some serious character...

Finally, let's look at C minor seventh flat five as a **"D"** shape in **Example 16e**:

Example 16e: C Minor 7 b5 Using "D" Shape

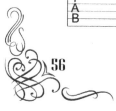

Notice again here that we have reduced the chord down to four voices. Also, pay attention to how this chord has the same order of pitches and spacing as the "**A**" shape chord, just played an octave higher and with the root on the D string.

Hey, look! Here's a map of all the minor seventh flat five CAGED voicings on the fretboard:

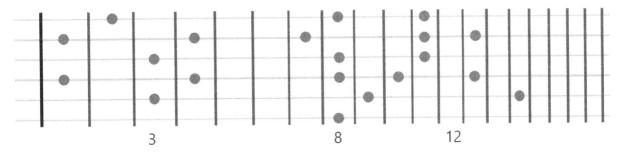

Some Example Chord Progressions:

CAGED Major and Minor Shapes

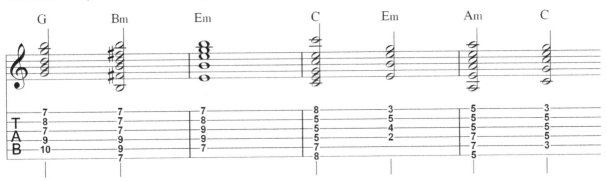

CAGED Major and Minor Shapes

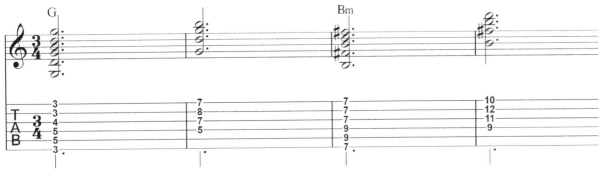

CAGED Major, Minor, and Dominant 7 Shapes

CAGED Major, Minor, Dominant, Minor 7b5 Shapes

In Conclusion

Great work! You made it through Level 2!

I'd suggest taking a breather here. Allow your brain to integrate the concepts. Don't overload yourself with too much at once.

Before going on, make sure you have a clear picture of how these different shapes fit together. Be sure you can identify the roots of these chords and that you feel comfortable moving them through all twelve keys.

Take a look at the Chord Dictionary for more information or if you're stuck!

LEVEL 3:
Inversions

Intro:

Hello again! You have now reached Level 3—that's no small feat! I admire your determination and consistency! After all, those are two qualities essential to your success and progress as a musician!

You must be determined; no one is going to practice for you. You must be consistent; if your practice is sporadic then you won't earn the steady progress that will turn you into a great guitarist!

So, you are now ready for Level 3: **Inversions.**

What is an inversion? When something is inverted, that usually means it is flipped upside down, or backwards, or mirrored in some way.

In music, when we talk about inversions, we refer to shifting the order of the pitches in a chord.

In this level, we'll learn about some basic inversions of major and minor chords, how they are constructed, and a few different chord shapes for you to play around with.

Hopefully you find some connections between the materials in this section and the chord shapes and theory you have learned in the previous two sections! Let us begin.

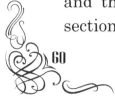

LEVEL 3 KEYWORDS

inversions, root position, first inversion, second inversion, slash chords

---

Major Triad Inversions

Remember from Level 1, the formula for a major triad is **1-3-5**, or in the key of C, we spell it C-E-G. We call this order of pitches **root position**.

So, what happens if, instead of starting with the root, we build the chord from the *third* tone? The formula then becomes **3-5-1**, or in the key of C, E-G-C. We call this order of pitches **first inversion**.

To take things a step further, if we start with the *fifth* tone, the formula becomes **5-1-3**, or in the key of C, G-C-E. We call this order of pitches **second inversion**.

To summarize: we have three possible inversions of a triad: root position (1-3-5) , first inversion (3-5-1) , and second inversion (5-1-3) .

Let's look below at **Example 1** for some visual representation:

Example 1: Major Triad Inversions

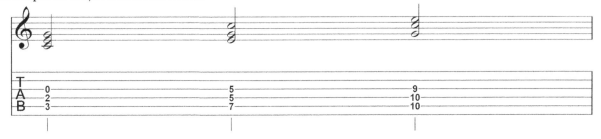

Can you see visually in this example how we basically take the lowest tone of the chord and shift it up one octave to make the inversion?

In the first chord, the bottom tone is 'C' and to make the first inversion, we shift 'C' up one octave so it is now the highest voice in the chord.

Same concept for the second inversion: we shift the lowest voice 'E' up one octave so it becomes the highest voice in the second inversion. Make sense?

Let us now look at the inversions for minor triads. We essentially follow the same steps; however, there is one difference.

Remember from Level 1, the formula for a minor triad is **1-b3-5**, or in the key of C, C-Eb-G. This is the root position triad. First inversion is spelled **b3-5-1** or Eb-G-C, and the second inversion is spelled **5-1-b3** or G-C-Eb.

Take a look below at the examples on the fretboard:

Example 2: Minor Triad Inversions

So far so good? That's it for the theory of inversions right now. Take a look at these examples of chords below. See if you can find where these triad shapes fit into the CAGED shapes from Level 2. Like magic, everything connects together. It's also important to memorize where the roots are in all of these chords.

Example 3: Major Triad Voicing #1 with Inversions

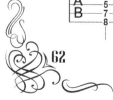

Notice the pattern of the root motion here. In the root position chord, the root is on the low E string. In the first inversion chord, the root is on the D string; in the second inversion chord, the root is on the A string.

Example 4: Major Triad Voicing #2 with Inversions

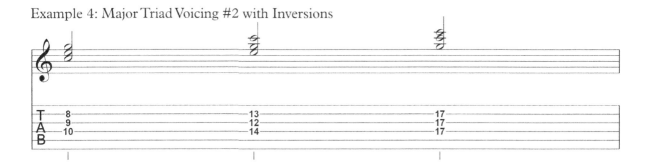

Do you see how these shapes fit into the CAGED shapes from Level 2? Particularly clear is the second inversion chord here very closely resembles the "**A**" shape CAGED chord, right?

See if you can find the other connections...

Example 5: Major Triad Voicing #3 with Inversions

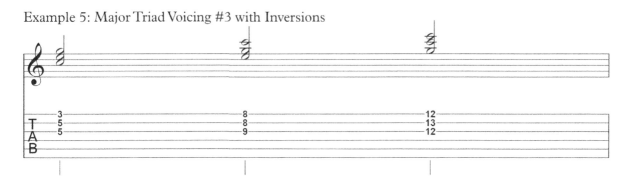

Now you've seen all the triad shapes played on three strings and all of their inversions. There are some other possibilities for voicing these chords. We call them spread triads, and we'll learn more about them in Level 8.

Until then, see if you can memorize these shapes—and if you're feeling ambitious, find some more and different ways to voice them!

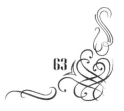

Minor Triad Inversions

Don't forget about all the different minor shapes! We accomplish them by using the same method:

Example 6: Minor Triad Voicing #1 with Inversions

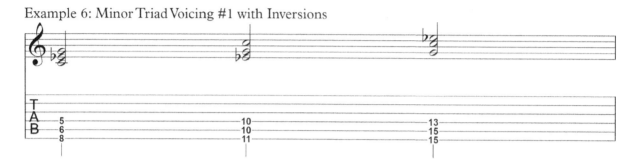

Do you see here how the root position chord in **Example 6** closely resembles the minor "**G**" shape CAGED chord?

Example 7: Minor Triad Voicing #2 with Inversions

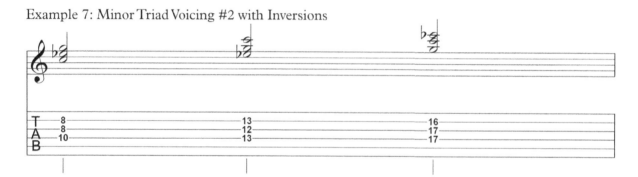

Notice how the second inversion chord in **Example 7** resembles a portion of the "**A**" shape minor chord?

Example 8: Minor Triad Voicing #3 with Inversions

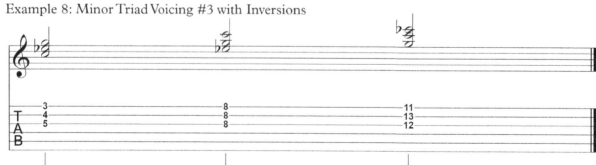

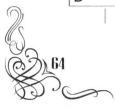

64

Chord Symbols for Inversions:

It is vital to recognize where an inversion is being called for in music. We have at least two different ways to commonly notate this; one of them is considered formal, the other is a bit more informal.

Remember from Level 1 how each degree of the major scale has a number associated with it? For instance, in the key of C: C is 1, D is 2, E is 3, etc.

In addition to these numbers, we also use roman numerals to analyze chords and chord progressions. In this system, C is **I**, D is **ii**, E is **iii**, F is **IV**, G is **V**, A is **vi**, and B is **vii**.

We use **upper case** roman numerals to denote **major** chords and **lower case** roman numerals to denote **minor** and **diminished** chords.

You might already be familiar with this system when it comes to denoting chord progressions. For example, if you see a progression **I-IV-V** in the key of C, that translates to C major — F major — G major, with all the chords in root position.

So what do you do if you want to invert any of these chords? In this system, we use the symbol I^6 to indicate a first inversion triad. The superscript 6 refers to the interval of a sixth that is created by the bottom voice and the top voice of a chord when we move to first inversion.

For the second inversion, we use the symbol I^6_4. The 6 again refers to the interval of a sixth created between the bottom and top voices of the chord in second inversion, and the 4 refers to the interval of a fourth created by the bottom voice and the middle voice of the chord in second inversion.

Still with me? Essentially, we have the roman numeral for the chord followed by some series of numbers that define the interval structure of the chord. Very formal. You would see this in your music theory class.

More informally, you would see something like **C/E** or **C/G** to indicate first and second inversion chords. We call this system **slash chords**—and no, not because Slash plays them all the time...

Slash chords are a shorthand method to indicate what the chord is (C) and what the bottom voice is (E). So if we see C/E, that means we play a C major chord with E as the bottom voice, aka first inversion.

If we see C/G that means we play a C major chord with G as the bottom voice, aka second inversion.

This more informal system is what you might see when playing with bands or on lead sheets or other sheet music.

Some Example Chord Progressions:

Example of Major and Minor Triad Inversions

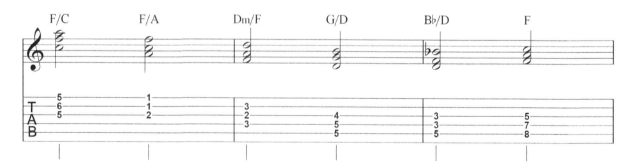

Examples of Major and Minor Triad Inversions

In Conclusion:

After applying these theories into real-world practice, you should hopefully begin to notice some patterns here between the different chords.

You may notice some overlap between all the chord shapes we've discussed so far. All these different systems for chords give us many options in the way that we can create expressive music. You can think of it like we're both drawing the same tree—only I'm using a pencil and you're using a marker. We achieve the same image in the end, but there are several ways of getting there.

Therefore, it's to your benefit to learn and understand all the different ways chords appear on the guitar fretboard and to build connections and meaning for yourself.

Oh, and don't forget all the chord shapes we've learned thus far only apply to standard tuning! Imagine what happens if you change the tuning of just one string…

LEVEL 4:
Symmetrical Chords

Intro:

Well my friend, I must say — I am most impressed you have made it this far! Of course I never doubted you... but now I know for certain that you are indeed committed to expanding your knowledge of the fretboard!

However, we now reach a crossroads in our journey...

"Yes, there are two paths you can go by, but in the long run" ... they both lead to the same location—because they're symmetrical!

That's right. We are now going to learn about what we call **symmetrical chords**, the diminished and augmented chords.

LEVEL 4 KEYWORDS

symmetrical chords, diminished chords, augmented chords, tertian harmony, quartal harmony, quintal harmony, cluster harmony, enharmonic equivalents

---

Diminished Seventh Chords:

Construction:

We briefly touched on the diminished triad in Level 1 when we built a diatonic chord scale in C major. We found that the diminished triad occurs only one time in the chord scale and that is on the seventh degree.

Recall that the formula for the diminished triad is **1-b3-b5**, or in the key of C, we spell it C-Eb-Gb. I told you we'd come back to it... Well, here we are!

As a reminder, the diatonic chord scale we built in Level 1 has major seventh chords, minor seventh chords, dominant seventh chords, and one minor seventh flat five chord naturally occurring in the scale.

The Harmonic Minor Scale

Do you see a diminished seventh chord anywhere in the major scale? No! So, where does the diminished seventh chord come from?

The diminished seventh chord first appears in the harmonic minor scale. Are you familiar with the harmonic minor scale? If not, take a look at **Example 1** below:

Example 1: C Harmonic Minor Scale

The harmonic minor scale has a very cool and dark sound to it—a definite necessity to have under your fingers!

The formula for this harmonic minor scale is **1-2-b3-4-5-b6-7-1**. We have a flat third and a flat sixth degree — but a *natural* seventh degree. The minor third interval between the flat sixth and the natural seventh is what sets us up for a diminished seventh chord.

If you take a look at **Example 2** below, you can see how it emerges from the scale:

Example 2: Diminished 7th Chord Inside C Harmonic Minor Scale

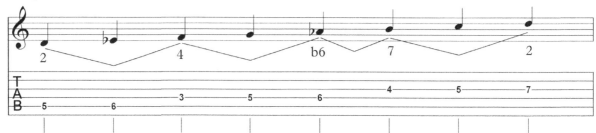

Remember from our experience building the seventh chords earlier that we stack thirds from the scale, or every other note, to uncover the chords.

This style of harmony is called "**tertian**" harmony — chords that are built in thirds. This is opposed to "**quartal**" harmony (chords built in fourths), or "**quintal**" harmony (chords built in fifths), or "**cluster**" harmony (chords that don't have an interval structure based on a scale).

We'll touch more on quartal harmony in Level 7.

Theory Time

You can see from Example 2 how the diminished seventh chord emerges from the **second** scale degree, from the **fourth** scale degree, the **flat sixth** scale degree, and the **natural seventh** scale degree.

The symmetrical nature of the diminished seventh chord implies that it can start from any tone of the chord; every tone of the diminished seventh chord can function as the root of the chord.

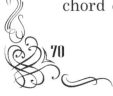

I know — what a headache! We'll talk more about its symmetrical nature in a moment; first let's look at its construction.

Example 3 shows a C diminished seventh chord:

Example 3: Diminished 7 Arpeggio and Chord

Compare this chord to the minor seventh flat five chord from Level 1. The only difference between this chord and the minor seventh flat five chord is that the seventh is one semitone lower, moving from 'Bb' to 'Bbb'.

Yes, you read that right. B double flat. Uh oh. Why Bbb and not just A natural, you might ask? Good question! That requires us to get down in the weeds a little bit...

Basically, the chord is a diminished *seventh* chord — so the intervals and names of pitches have to be in sync with the formula of the chord. The formula of the chord is **1-b3-b5-bb7**. So the bb7 in a C diminished seventh chord is B double flat.

We can't say the chord is spelled C-Eb-Gb-A, because A is the *sixth* degree of C, even though B double flat and A natural are **enharmonic equivalents** (the same pitch).

Make sense? You're right, it's kind of a nitty gritty detail—but the nitty gritty details are what sets the masters apart from the apprentices!

Intervals of the Diminished Seventh Chord

Let's continue excavating this diminished seventh chord and see what mysteries we can uncover.

See below in **Example 4**, the intervals of a C diminished seventh chord:

Example 4: Intervals of Diminished 7 Chord

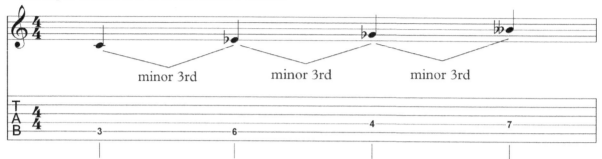

What do you notice about this chord? The most important thing to see is how each tone of the chord is a minor third away from the next. The diminished seventh chord is the first chord we have encountered that is built entirely from the same interval.

This means that the chord is symmetrical. We can start the chord from any tone of the chord and it will remain the same chord. C diminished seventh has the same notes as Eb diminished seventh, as Gb diminished seventh, and as Bbb diminished seventh.

Some Voicings

OK, enough theory for now — let's start practicing! Get your fingers around some of these diminished seventh voicings:

Example 5: C Diminished 7 Voicing #1

Example 5 is a classic guitar voicing for the diminished seventh chord on the top four strings. We've called it 'C' diminished seventh here, but remember that any chord tone can function as the root!

Example 6: C Diminished 7 Voicing #2

Example 6 shows another great and useful diminished seventh voicing on the middle four strings. We have again called this 'C' diminished seventh — and 'C' in the chord voicing is on the A string.

One more voicing for now:

Example 7: C Diminished 7 Voicing #3

Example 7 is one more classical voicing for a diminished seventh chord played on the lowest four strings of the guitar. Where is 'C' in this voicing? On the D string. Nice!

Take some time to play through all these voicings and practice jumping between the different string sets. What similarities do you notice between them?

The diminished seventh chord is symmetrical, but the tuning of the guitar is not. How does the standard tuning system affect the shape of these voicings as we move them through the different string sets? Think about it...

More On Symmetry

Are you starting to see the symmetry of this diminished seventh chord? Is the mist surrounding this enigmatic harmony beginning to lift?

Perhaps another exercise will help you better visualize this symmetry:

Example 8: The Symmetry of Minor Thirds

Practice this exercise from 'C' as it is written and also from every other 'C' you can find on the fretboard, then move it through all twelve keys. The patterns you find in it should be illuminating!

Practicing the different inversions of diminished seventh chords is another effective strategy to clarify the symmetry. Check out **Example 9** below:

Example 9: C Diminished 7 Inversions

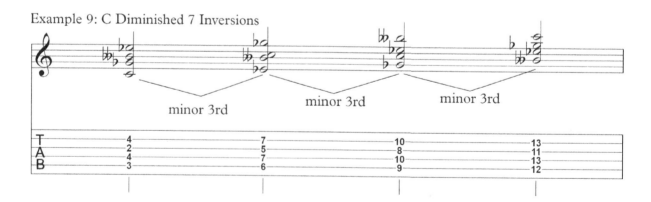

Do you see in the example how we maintain the same chord shape through the different inversions? And that all the inversions are a minor third apart, just as all the tones in the chord are a minor third apart? What do you make of this? How does this sound to you?

74

For your reference, here is a map of all the diminished seventh tones on the fretboard in the key of C (or Eb, Gb, or Bbb):

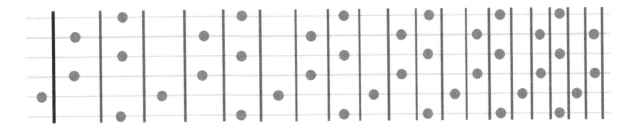

One last visual aid for the diminished seventh chord:

What is that wacky thing you might be thinking? That, my friend, are the four possible diminished seventh chords plotted on a pitch wheel! Crazy, right?! I *told you* the mysteries of music can be found all across the shapes, colors and nature around you!

I'll let that one sink in for a while...

Augmented Triads

Perhaps you've been thinking outside the box a little and have wondered if there's a chord built in major thirds? Well, my friend, you are precocious indeed!

We call a triad built in major thirds an **augmented triad**.

Example 10: C Augmented Arpeggio and Triad

We can see in **Example 10** the C augmented triad, spelled C-E-G#. Its formula is **1-3-#5**.

What transformation did we make to the major triad from Level 1 to build this augmented triad? Did I hear you say "raise the fifth scale degree"? Then you are correct!

Many interesting things happen when we augment the fifth. Take a look at **Example 11** below for a more detailed picture of the interval structure:

Example 11: Intervals of the Augmented Triad

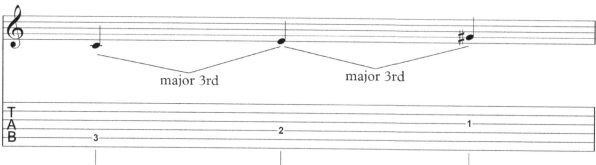

We can see here the augmented triad is built from **two major thirds,** as opposed to the series of minor thirds that composed the diminished triad and seventh chords.

If we go up another major third from 'G#' in the chord above, we reach 'C' again. This means that we can only have an augmented triad. There is no augmented seventh chord in the sense that there's a diminished seventh chord.

There are, for example, major seventh chords with an augmented fifth — but we refer to those as something else.

This fact is also significant because it means there are only four possible augmented chords: C-E-G#, Db-F-A, D-F#-A#, and Eb-G-B (and their enharmonic equivalents).

You can see them represented here visually on the pitch wheel:

You see the four separate triangles? Pretty mind blowing, huh?

The augmented chord is also intriguing because it forms an equilateral triangle on the pitch wheel. I know you didn't sign up for geometry class here, but I think it's an interesting visualization — and it reveals some of the transcendent information about music. Musical mysticism you might say...

OK, back to earth — here is an exercise to see the symmetry of the augmented chord on the fretboard:

Example 12: The Symmetry of Major Thirds

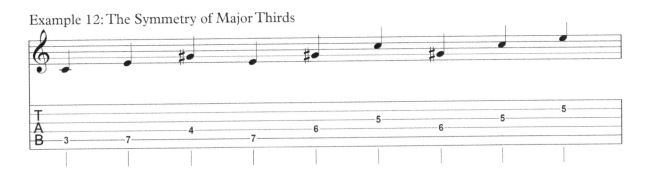

Like Example 8 previously, try practicing this exercise starting from 'C' as it's written and then from all the other 'C's you can find, and then finally through all twelve keys. This should help you gain a greater understanding of the symmetrical nature of the augmented chord!

Now that we've laid the theory foundation for the augmented triad, let's play through some different voicings.

Check out these voicings based on the lowest three strings:

Example 13: Augmented Triad Voicing #1 and Inversions

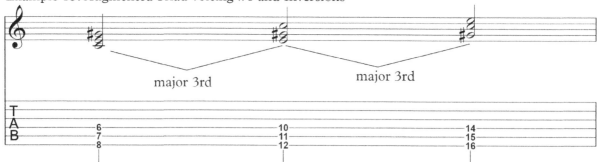

See how each of the inversions is a major third apart, just as the inversions of the diminished seventh chord were a minor third apart? Also, can you see how each chord is identical in shape, but we just reshuffle the order of the notes?

Like the diminished seventh chord, any tone of the augmented chord can function as the root, it just depends on how it's moving in the music.

Here are some examples of augmented chords starting from the A string:

Example 14: Augmented Triad Voicing #2 and Inversions

See how it's the same basic chord shape as the voicings in the previous example? That is no mere coincidence!

See if you can connect these voicings starting from the A string with the voicings from **Example 13**.

In **Example 15**, the shape shifts slightly due to the tuning of the guitar:

Example 15: Augmented Triad Voicing #3 and Inversions

The voicings in this example start on the 10th fret of the D string and continue up above the 12th fret. See if you can find the locations of the 1st and 2nd inversions one octave lower. Hint: the 2nd and 6th frets would be helpful...

One more set. Check out these voicings starting from the G string.

Example 16: Augmented Triad Voicing #4 and Inversions

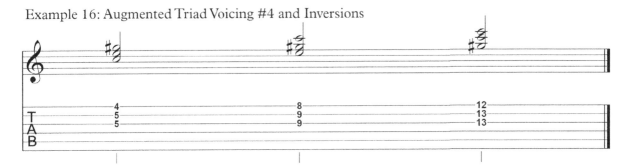

Can you connect all of these voicings from each group of strings in a line? Maybe this map of the augmented tones on the fretboard will help you visualize what I mean:

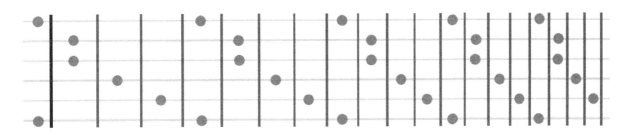

Some Example Chord Progressions:

Example of Diminished 7 Chord

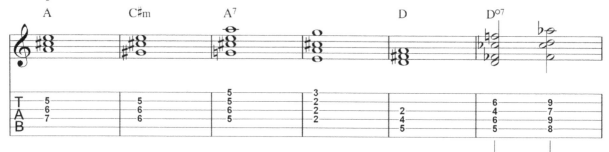

Example of Diminished 7 Chord

Example of Augmented Triads

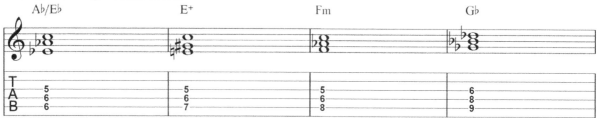

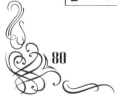

In Conclusion:

The guitar fretboard is designed in such a way that symmetrical figures are somewhat intuitive. If you imagine notes on the fretboard as points on a graph or a grid, then it's easy to "draw" shapes and create interesting patterns that could not be so easily generated using "traditional" methods of music theory.

The diminished seventh and augmented chords present a region of traditional music theory that is symmetrical; my hope is you have learned how to visualize these patterns on the fretboard and see how they can be used in music to elicit their own individual emotional responses.

LEVEL 5:
Extensions

Intro:

So you're still here, huh? You *are* bold!

Are you starting to see your efforts pay off? You've come a long way since we met at Level 1—and it shows! You have made your way through triads, diatonic seventh chords, inversions, and symmetrical chords.

However... thus far all the concepts we've discussed take place inside the distance of one octave. But the world of music does not end at the octave!

In this section we will dive into **extensions** — the world *above* the octave!

LEVEL 5 KEYWORDS:

extensions, triad stacking, extended harmony, rootless voicings

---

What Are Extensions?

In music theory, extensions are simply the chord tones above the octave. Check out the C major scale played over two octaves in **Example 1**:

Example 1: 2 Octave C Major Scale

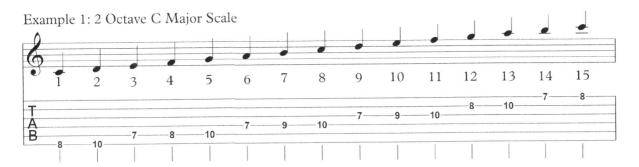

When we pass the octave in the major scale, we use the integers **9, 10, 11, 12, 13, 14,** and **15** to refer to the tones of the scale. 9 is the same pitch as 2; however, it is one octave higher. The same is true for the other pitches: 10 is the same pitch as 3, 11 is the same pitch as 4, etc.

Due to the nature of our harmony system built in thirds (remember the name for that... **tertian harmony!**), we most often encounter the extensions 9, 11, and 13. Review **Example 2** below for a visual representation of this:

Example 2: Stacking Thirds to Build Extensions

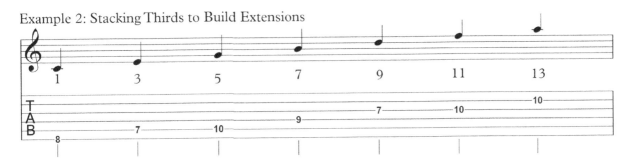

All we've done here is continue to skip up every other tone in the C major scale. If we added one more jump up from 'A', the highest pitch in Example 2, we would reach 'C' again. It's also interesting that all 7 pitches of the C major scale are represented here.

Triad Stacking to Build Extended Harmony

Okay... I promise I won't scare you off with anything too complex. Let's uncover a way we can build chords with these extensions using the triads we learned previously. This technique is called **triad stacking,** and it's an interesting way to construct **extended harmony** — or chords with extensions.

Major Chords

Let's first discuss the major chords, beginning with the major seventh chord. Take a gander at **Example 3**:

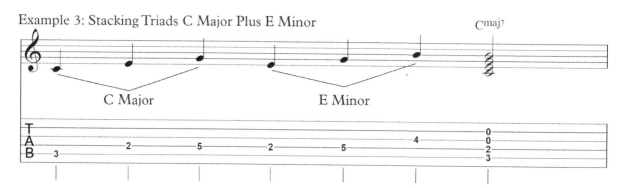

Example 3: Stacking Triads C Major Plus E Minor

In this example, we take a C major triad and add an E minor triad on top to build a C major seventh chord. The C major seventh chord contains both a C major triad and an E minor triad. What do you think of that? Pretty cool, huh?

OK, that was too easy. What do you think happens if we put a G major triad on top of the C major triad? Head on over to **Example 4** below to find out:

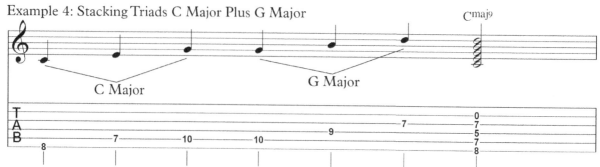

Example 4: Stacking Triads C Major Plus G Major

The C major triad and G major triad share a common tone of 'G'; when added together, they form a C major ninth chord. C major ninth means we have all the tones of the basic C major seventh chord (C-E-G-B) and then add the ninth tone, 'D'.

As we progress through these extended harmonies, you'll find that most of them have too many notes to be played on a guitar in standard tuning.

The best strategy to overcome this is to ~~grow extra fingers~~ err, I mean omit or substitute certain voices as we've discussed previously. If necessary, we can remove the root and the fifth from any of these chords.

This C major ninth chord in Example 4 is playable using the given tab. However, the chords in tab at the end of the following examples are largely not playable; they're given primarily as a visual reference to demonstrate the triad stacking technique.

Later in this section, there will be three examples of voicings given for each quality and extension—and make sure to consult the Chord Dictionary where more examples are given!

OK, let us continue…

How can we stack two triads to build a major eleventh chord? Check out **Example 5** for the details:

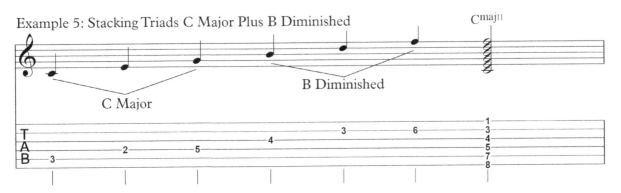

Example 5: Stacking Triads C Major Plus B Diminished

This is the first extended harmony we've learned where the two triads used do not share any common tones. If we add a B diminished triad to a C major triad, the resulting chord is called C major eleventh spelled C-E-G-B-D-F.

How does this chord sound to you? A major chord with a diminished chord inside of it? How strange this is becoming...

We'll cover one more extended harmony on the major seventh chord: the wonderful major thirteenth. How do we use triads to build a major thirteenth chord, you ask? Well, for this harmony, we need to use *three* triads. Check it out in **Example 6**:

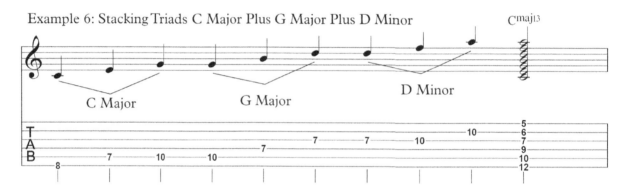

Example 6: Stacking Triads C Major Plus G Major Plus D Minor

We're stacking G major and D minor triads on a C major triad to build C major thirteenth. Remember, major thirteenth means we have all the chord tones (C-E-G-B) plus the extensions (D-F-A).

This is a solid and dense chord that covers a lot of sonic space.

So much space, in fact, that it can't be played on the guitar! The tab written in Example 6 does not include the root 'C' and instead starts from the 12th fret on the low E string.

Great work! We've learned how to stack triads to build extended harmonies on the major seventh chord. You are turning into a true music theorist!

Minor Chords

Let's now turn our attention to some minor chords. We'll follow a similar path as we did for the major harmonies by first stacking triads to build a minor seventh chord. See **Example 7** below:

Example 7: Stacking Triads C Minor Plus Eb Major

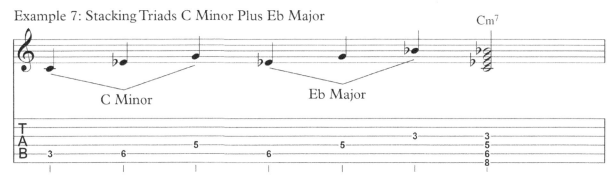

In this example, we have added Eb major to C minor to build C minor seventh. The C minor seventh chord contains both a C minor triad and an Eb major triad.

Notice here, as in Example 3 previously, the qualities of triads used mirrors the quality of interval that defines the chord. A minor chord is composed of a minor third followed by a major third. A minor seventh chord is constructed from a minor triad followed by a major triad.

Make sense? In Example 1, we found a major triad plus a minor triad equals a major seventh chord, just as a major triad is built from a major third followed by a minor third. What do you make of this?

Continuing on, what two triads do you think we'll use to build a C minor ninth chord? Remember C minor ninth is spelled C-Eb-G-Bb-D. Check out **Example 8** below for the answer:

Example 8: Stacking Triads C Minor Plus G Minor

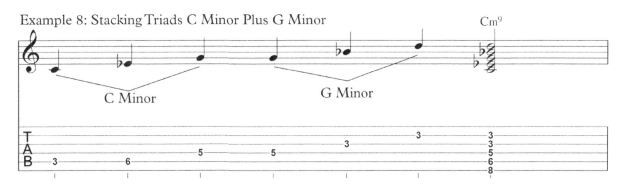

This is very similar to how we built the major ninth harmony. In this example, we add G minor to C minor to build C minor ninth. The C minor and G minor triads share 'G' as a common tone, and the G minor triad gives us 'Bb' (the seventh), and 'D' (the ninth).

To build the minor eleventh chord, we add a Bb major triad to a C minor triad as shown in **Example 9**:

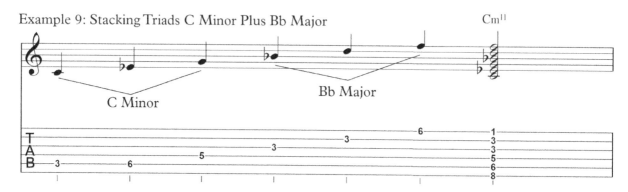

Example 9: Stacking Triads C Minor Plus Bb Major

See here how we have tones **1-b3-5** represented in the C minor triad, and tones **b7-9-11** represented by the Bb major chord?

One more to check out here:

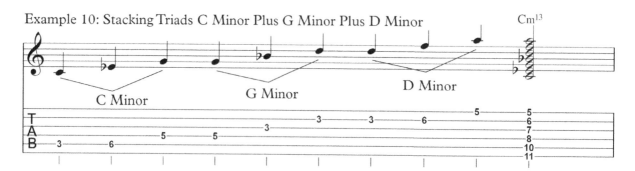

Example 10: Stacking Triads C Minor Plus G Minor Plus D Minor

In **Example 10**, we see the C minor thirteenth chord built by stacking C minor, G minor, and D minor triads. The formula for this chord is **1-b3-5-b7-9-11-13**. Woah!

Like the major thirteenth example previously, the tab for Example 10 starts from Eb, on the 11th fret of the low E string.

Wonderful! How do you feel? You have now learned how to build extended minor harmonies by stacking triads!

What can we conclude from this so far? Have you noticed any patterns developing in the triads used to build these chords? Keep studying the relationships and we will unpack them more at the end of the section.

Dominant chords:

Finally, we reach the dominant chords. Dominant chords present some interesting opportunities with extensions, which we'll discuss further in the next section. Let us lay the groundwork here.

First, let's build a basic dominant seventh chord from triads. Check out **Example 11** below:

Example 11: Stacking Triads C Major Plus E Diminished

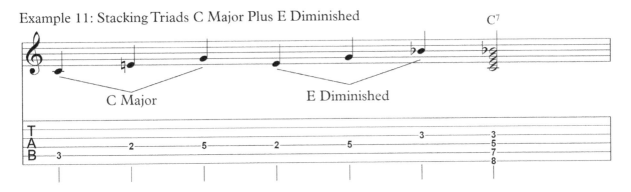

Here we add an E diminished triad to a C major triad to create C dominant seventh. The C major triad and the E diminished triad have two tones in common, 'E' and 'G', and the E diminished triad adds the tone 'Bb' to give us C-E-G-Bb — or C dominant seventh.

In **Example 12**, we see how stacking a C major triad and a G minor triad gives us C dominant ninth:

Example 12: Stacking Triads C Major Plus G Minor

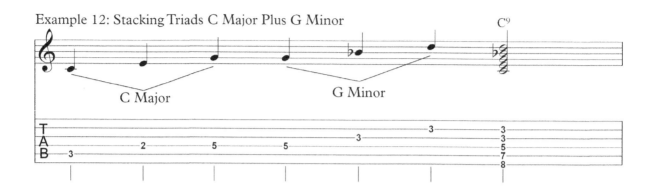

So far, all of the ninth harmonies have been built with some quality of a 'G' triad. It's reasonable to conclude that a 9th harmony can be built by a triad with a given root and a triad a fifth above the root. Almost sounds like a geometry theorem or something...

What about the dominant eleventh chord? The two eleventh harmonies we have learned so far have been built on some quality of a 'B' triad, whether that is a B diminished triad or a Bb major triad. What do you anticipate to be the case with the dominant eleventh extension? Check out **Example 13** for the answer:

Example 13: Stacking Triads C Major Plus Bb Major

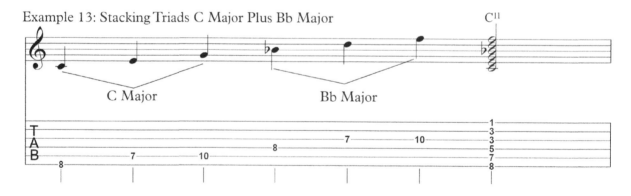

I don't know about you, but I wasn't expecting this...

The C dominant eleventh harmony is built from a C major triad and a Bb major triad—two major triads a minor seventh interval apart. This is interesting because the dominant seventh chord is defined by the major third (both triads are major) and by the flat seventh scale degree (both triads are a flat seventh apart). How strange!

Let's check out one more extension before we dive into some examples of voicings. Like the thirteen harmonies we've already covered, the dominant thirteenth extension is built from three triads. Refer to **Example 14** below:

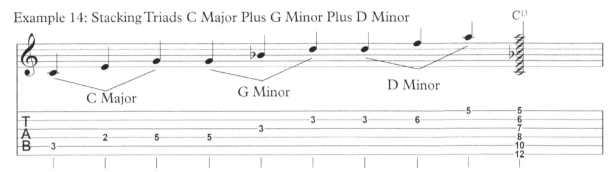

Example 14: Stacking Triads C Major Plus G Minor Plus D Minor

We build the C dominant thirteenth harmony from stacking C major, G minor, and D minor triads. Notice that these three triads are all a perfect fifth (7 semitones) apart.

This chord is too big to play on the guitar without some modification; the tab in the example above starts on the 12th fret of the low E string, and it does not cover the root.

Voicings!

The moment you've been waiting for has finally arrived! We are now going to review some practical examples of voicing shapes for these extended harmonies.

Major Voicings

Example 15 offers some major ninth voicings:

Example 15: Three Major 9 Voicings

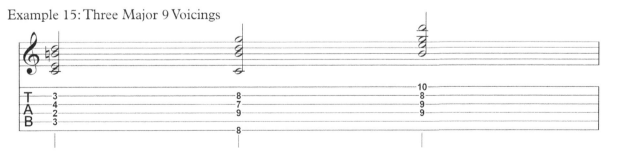

The first chord has its root on the A string and includes tones **1-3-7-9**. We have omitted the fifth from the chord.

The second chord has its root on the low E string and includes tones **1-5-7-9**. We've omitted the third from this chord. How did we do that, you ask? Well, we are guitar players — and we can do whatever we want!

The third chord in the example has no root! It includes tones **3-5-7-9**.

When learning to use these **rootless voicings** you should find some way to visually relate the shape to the root, even though the root isn't present in the shape. You can relate this shape to 'C' on the 10th fret of the D string, or to 'C' on the 8th fret of the high E string.

Check out **Example 16** for some major eleventh voicings:

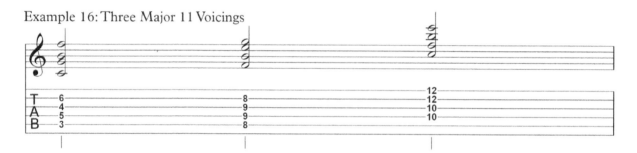

Example 16: Three Major 11 Voicings

The first chord has its root on the A string and includes tones **1-5-7-11**. We have substituted the eleventh for the third in the chord. Does this chord look similar to any other chords we've learned so far?

The second chord is a rootless voicing. We have tones **11-7-3-5**, in that order. Where is this chord in relation to the root 'C'? We can visualize this shape connected to 'C' on the 8th fret of the low E string, or to 'C' on the 10th fret of the D string.

The third chord has its root on the 10th fret of the D string and includes tones **1-11-7-3**. Do you think this chord sounds clearly defined, or does it have an ambiguous nature?

Example 17 gives us some major thirteenth voicings:

Example 17: Three Major 13 Voicings

The first chord again has its root on the A string and is spelled C-E-A-D, a variation on the major ninth chord we learned in Example 15. We replaced the fifth in that chord with the thirteenth in this chord.

The second chord has its root on the low E string and includes tones **1-7-3-13**. There's a lot of weight to this voicing; it's a great shape to know!

The third chord has its root on the D string and is spelled C-G-A-D or **1-5-13-9**. See how this is a variation on the "D" shape major seventh we learned in Level 3?

Minor Voicings:

Look at **Example 18** for some cool minor ninth voicings:

Example 18: Three Minor 9 Voicings

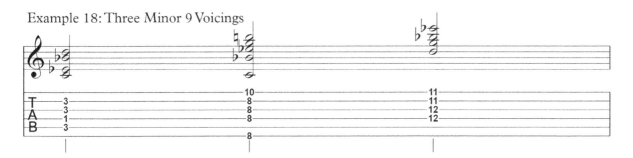

This first voicing in this example is a very useful minor ninth voicing with the root on the A string. It contains the **root**, the **flat third**, the **flat seventh**, and the **ninth**.

The second voicing has its root on the low E string and is spelled C-Bb-Eb-G-D, with the ninth played in the high E string with your pinky. This chord requires some flexibility — so stretch those fingers!

The third shape here is a rootless voicing spelled D-G-Bb-Eb. We can associate this chord with the root 'C' on the 10th fret of the D string, or with 'C' on the 13th fret of the B string.

Check out **Example 19** for some interesting minor eleventh voicings:

Example 19: Three Minor 11 Voicings

This first voicing again has its root on the A string (are you noticing a pattern here?) and is spelled C-F-Bb-Eb. This chord alludes to the topic of Level 7, **Quartal Harmony**. As you may recall, quartal harmony refers to chords that are built in fourths.

The second voicing in Example 19 has its root on the low E string and is spelled C-Bb-Eb-F. Pay attention to the major second interval at the top of the chord between Eb and F. How does this tension affect the feeling of the chord?

The third voicing in this example has its root on the D string and is spelled C-G-Bb-F. This is a great ambient voicing; it sounds fresh and modern—and it's also interesting to note that it is composed of two perfect fifths a minor third apart. Woah!

Check out **Example 20** for some hip minor thirteenth voicings:

Example 20: Three Minor 13 Voicings

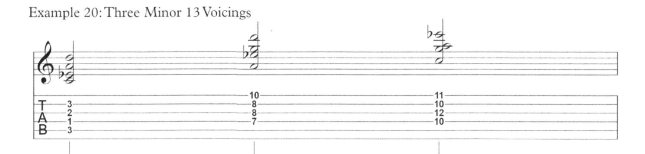

The first voicing has its root on the A string and is spelled C-Eb-A-D. This voicing sounds tense and dark to me. Do you notice the minor chord quality?

The second voicing does not contain the root. It is spelled A-Eb-G-D, starting from 'A' on the 7th fret of the D string. We can connect this voicing with 'C' on the 8th fret of the high E string. This is a voicing shape that can function in a number of different ways, and I encourage you to experiment with it!

The third voicing has its root on the D string and is spelled C-G-A-Eb. I love voicings like this that have an interval of a second inside of them. Notice this shape is very similar to the "A" shape minor seventh CAGED voicing.

Dominant Voicings:

Take a look at **Example 21** for some dominant ninth shapes:

Example 21: Three Dominant 9 Voicings

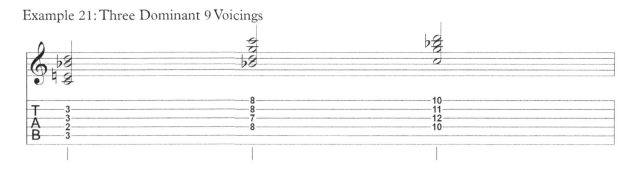

The first voicing in Example 21 has its root on the A string. This is a common dominant ninth voicing; I suggest you quickly commit it to memory, as you will likely use it all the time!

The second chord in this example is the same shape as the first chord, only played on the top four strings. It is spelled Bb-D-G-C with the root on the high E string. Another very useful chord.

The third chord here has its root on the D string and is spelled C-G-Bb-D. We could also think of this chord as a G minor triad on top of 'C'. What do you make of this harmony without the third in it? Does it sound clearly like a dominant chord, or is it a little more subdued?

Check out **Example 22** for some dominant eleventh voicings:

Example 22: Three Dominant 11 Voicings

What difference do you see between the first voicing in Example 22 and the first minor eleventh voicing in Example 19? All we've done is change the Eb on the 4th fret of the B string in Example 19 to an E natural on the fifth fret of the B string in Example 22. Neat, right?

The second voicing in this example is a rootless voicing spelled F-Bb-D-G, meaning it contains the **fifth**, the **flat seventh**, the **ninth**, and the **eleventh**. We can associate this chord with 'C' on the 8th fret of the low and high E strings.

The third voicing in this example has its root on the D string; unlike previous examples, it includes a note 'F' on the 8th fret of the A string. This chord is spelled F-C-E-Bb, meaning it contains the **root**, the **third**, the **flat seventh**, and the **eleventh**.

One more round! See **Example 23** for some dominant thirteenth voicings:

Example 23: Three Dominant 13 Voicings

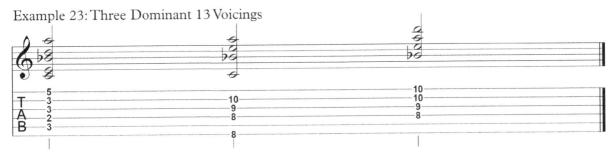

The first voicing should remind you of this second minor thirteenth voicing. Here, the root is on the A string — but the rest of the shape is identical. This chord can be a dominant thirteenth chord when we have the root on the A string, or it can be a minor thirteenth chord when positioned as in Example 20. What other uses for this chord can you find?

The second voicing is a classic dominant thirteenth voicing I suggest you memorize quickly. The root is on the low E string and includes the **root**, the **third**, the **flat seventh** and the **thirteenth**.

The third voicing is a rootless voicing spelled Bb-E-A-D, so it contains the **third**, the **flat seventh**, the **ninth**, and the **thirteenth**. It's a variation on the second voicing in Example 23, only played on the top four strings instead of spread across 5 strings. Likewise, it is very useful. Try to associate this chord with the root 'C' on the 8th fret of the high E string or the 8th fret of the low E string.

Some Example Chord Progressions:

Example of Dominant 9 Chord

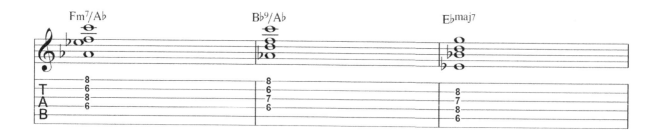

Example of Minor 11 and Dominant 13 Chords on Minor Blues

Example of Major 9, Minor 9, Dominant 13 Chords

Am⁷⁽♭⁵⁾   D⁷   Gm⁹

```
T---5-----------5-----------5-----------8------
   -4-----------3-----------3-----------6------
A--5-----------5-----------3-----------7------
   -5-----------4-----------3-----------7------
B----------------------------------------------
```

In Conclusion:

Nice work, my friend! I hope your mind is feeling sufficiently extended!

To summarize: Extensions are essentially chord tones above the octave. The most common extensions are the **ninth**, **eleventh**, and **thirteenth**.

These extensions are naturally occurring in the scale because of our tertian harmony system, and we can also derive them by stacking triads together.

There are actually many other options for stacking triads that we didn't discuss in this Level. What do you think happens to our extensions if we use some other types of triads?

For instance, what if we stack a B major triad on top of a C major triad? What happens to the extensions then? How do we describe the sound of that chord? How do we play that chord on the guitar?

Keep reading through Level 6 to find out...

LEVEL 6:
Altered Chords

Intro:

Congratulations, my friend: You are well on your way to becoming a chord master! This is no easy feat to accomplish! I'm impressed by your determination to reach this point (assuming you actually read the other chapters?!).

> ### LEVEL 6 KEYWORDS:
>
> *altered chords*

What is an Altered Chord?

Ready or not, we now will dive into **altered chords**.

What are altered chords, you ask? In their simplest sense, altered chords are dominant seventh chords that have an alteration on the extensions.

Remember from Level 5, we have three extensions that are commonly voiced in chords: the ninth, the eleventh, and the thirteenth. When we talk about altered chords, we're referring to chords that have either a **flat or sharp ninth**, a **sharp eleventh**, or a **flat thirteenth**.

You may also see **flat or sharp fifth**—or you may see alterations on **major seventh** or **minor seventh** chords, but we'll only be discussing the altered dominant seventh chords right now.

Altered Dominant Ninth Chords

First, we'll check out alterations on the ninth extension. There's two possibilities here. Check out C dominant seventh flat ninth in **Example 1**:

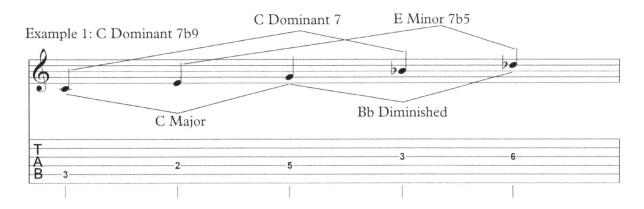

Yikes! I know, crazy right? What's up with all those lines in there? Let's dissect this a little bit...

The formula for C dominant seventh flat ninth is **1-3-5-b7-b9**—or in this case, C-E-G-Bb-Db. We can also see this chord as a series of triads stacked, like we explored in Level 5.

C dominant seventh flat ninth is composed of a C major triad and a Bb diminished triad. Cool, right? We can also see it as a C dominant seventh chord plus an E minor seventh flat five chord.

Math! Harmony! Huzzah!

What does this chord sound like to you? Let's look at an example of this chord in some music. Here in **Example 2**, we find E dominant seventh flat ninth in context of a chord progression in A minor:

Example 2: Dominant 7b9

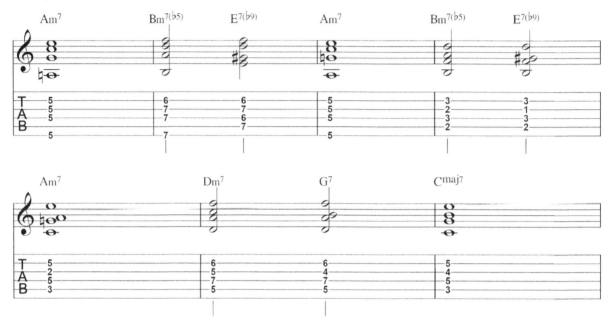

There are two different shapes for E dominant seventh flat ninth in this example. I hope you recognize both of them!

This first one is a variation on the dominant ninth chord we learned in Level 5. All we did was flat the ninth degree on the B string. Easy, right?

The second one is a straight up diminished seventh chord just like the shape we learned in Level 4. How is that possible?

Remember earlier in this chapter, we found that a dominant seventh flat ninth chord can be thought of as a diminished seventh chord stacked on a dominant seventh chord? That means anytime we see a dominant seventh flat ninth chord, we can think of it as a diminished seventh chord on the flat ninth degree.

For instance, if we have C dominant seventh flat ninth, we can think of Db diminished seventh because Db is the flat ninth degree of C.

There's one other option for altering the ninth degree — and that is to flat the ninth.

Refer to **Example 3** for some details about this harmony:

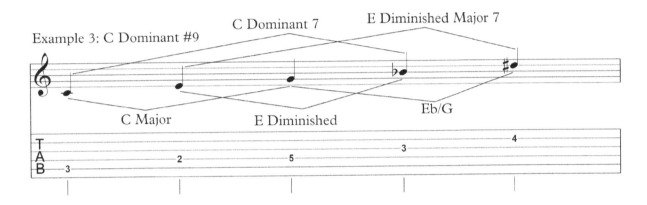

The formula for a dominant seventh sharp ninth is **1-3-5-b7-#9**, or in this case, we spell it C-E-G-Bb-D#.

This chord is a little less straightforward than the dominant seventh flat ninth chord and doesn't appear in a scale as clearly. It's made its mark on contemporary music primarily through blues, funk, and jazz music—and its connection with the minor pentatonic scale.

Here is a great example of this chord:

Example 4: Dominant 7 #9

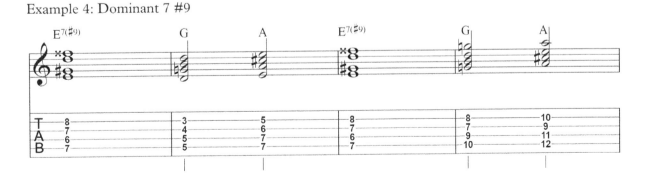

This voicing is a variation on one of the dominant ninth shapes we learned in Level 5. All we did was raise the ninth tone on the B string one half step. You can find some other more interesting voicings for this harmony in the Chord Dictionary.

Alterations on the Eleventh:

How do you feel about the number 11? How did the minor eleventh chord harmony we learned in Level 5 make you feel?

If we flat the eleventh, we just end up with the third, right? So that means our only option is to *raise* the eleventh. This brings us to the dominant seventh sharp eleventh harmony.

Have a listen in **Example 5**:

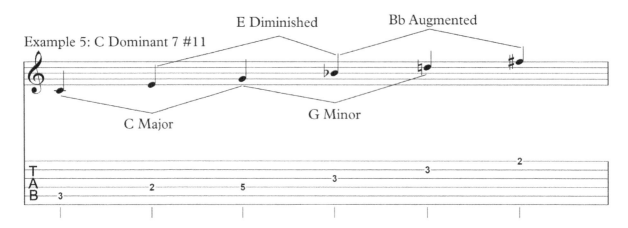

What can you discern from this example? Can you see how C dominant seventh sharp eleventh is built from C major, E diminished, G minor, and Bb augmented triads? (That's a mouthful!)

The formula for this harmony is **1-3-5-b7-9-#11**—or in this case, spelled C-E-G-Bb-D-F#.

Do you sense the unresolved tension? Or maybe you feel comfortable in the tension? Personally, I like to think of these more dissonant harmonies as

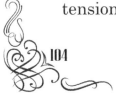

something to be learned and absorbed as a positive force, not as something dark or dissonant as a negative concept.

Here's an example of a dominant seventh sharp eleventh in a classic chord progression:

Example 6: Dominant 7#11

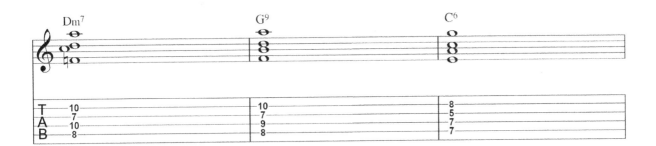

What do you notice about the two voicings for D dominant seventh sharp eleventh in **Example 6**?

The same shape, a major third apart, you say?? Well, look at you! You are becoming very insightful, indeed!

Yes, it's true — they are the same shape a major third apart. The first voicing has the root on the 5th fret of the A string and the second shape is a rootless voicing.

What do you think happens if you move the voicing up another major third? You'd make D dominant seventh sharp eleventh flat thirteenth.

Woah. We won't be touching on chords with two alterations in them, but it's nice to know they exist!

You can find some more voicings for dominant seventh sharp eleventh chords in the Chord Dictionary.

Alterations on the Thirteenth

Are you ready for this? One more alteration we'll touch on is the flat thirteenth. Check out C dominant seventh flat thirteenth in **Example 7** below:

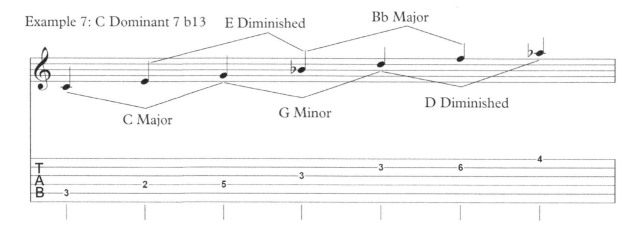

Example 7: C Dominant 7 b13

Yikes! What sort of tangled nightmare is that?

The formula for the dominant seventh flat thirteenth harmony is, brace yourself: **1-3-5-b7-9-11-b13**. Huge! In this case, we spell it C-E-G-Bb-D-F-Ab. Massive.

How are you going to play all those tones in one chord on the guitar!? Check out **Example 8** for some tips:

Example 8: Dominant 7b13

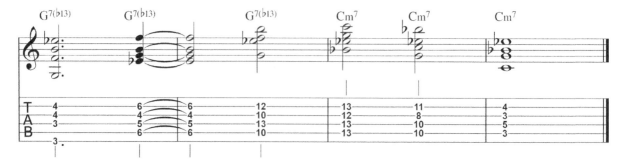

Here we find a G dominant seventh flat thirteenth in the classic tune "Stella By Starlight".

There are three voicings in this example — all three different shapes. The first has its root on the low E string and is a variation on the dominant thirteenth shape we learned in Level 5.

The root of the second voicing is found on the D string. This shape resembles the augmented triad we learned in Level 4 with the addition of the seventh degree (in this harmony) on the B string.

The third voicing is rooted on the A string and resembles one of the dominant seventh shapes we learned in Level 1. We've raised the fifth tone, 'D', found on the 12th fret of the D string, to 'E' on the thirteenth fret of the 'D' string.

Conclusion

In summation, an altered chord is simply a harmony that has alterations made to the extensions of the chord. That means we either **flat or sharp the ninth, sharp the eleventh**, or **flat the thirteenth**.

We do have chords with more than one alteration. For example, you might find a dominant seventh sharp eleventh flat thirteenth chord. Or a dominant seventh flat ninth sharp ninth chord...

I'm sure that, with all this advanced musical theory knowledge you've obtained, you'll know exactly what to do in those situations!

LEVEL 7:
Quartal Harmony

Intro:

Do you remember in Level 4 when I mentioned the term "quartal harmony"?

Well, guess what my friend? The time has finally arrived! We're going to dig deeper into the topic of quartal harmony.

Quartal harmony refers to chords that are built in a series of **fourths**, as opposed to the other chords we have learned so far, which are all stacked in thirds.

Remember, we call chords built in thirds tertian harmony or tertiary harmony.

LEVEL 7 KEYWORDS:

quartal harmony, perfect fourth, augmented fourth, tri-tone, planing

---

Two Types of Fourths

Before we dive into some chord shapes, it's important we learn about two types of fourths: the **perfect fourth** and the **augmented fourth**.

108

In **Example 1** below, we find these two types of fourths in the C major scale:

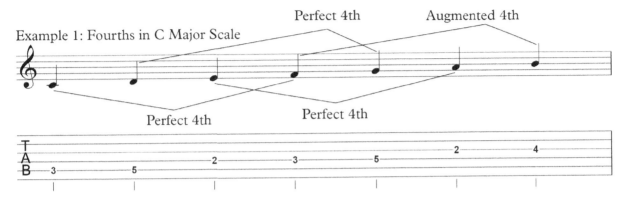

Example 1: Fourths in C Major Scale

As you can see here, the most common type of fourth in the scale is the perfect fourth. The augmented fourth only occurs one time, from 'F' to 'B'.

You're probably already familiar with this interval known as a **tri-tone**.

Check out **Example 2** for more detail about these fourths:

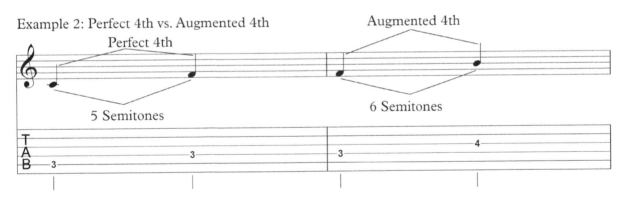

Example 2: Perfect 4th vs. Augmented 4th

We can see in this example that the perfect fourth is composed of 5 semitones and the augmented fourth is composed of 6 semitones. This distinction becomes important when we build a quartal diatonic chord scale.

Quartal Harmony in the Minor Pentatonic Scale

Before jumping into quartal harmony in the major scale, we will first learn some quartal chord shapes derived from the minor pentatonic scale. I trust you are familiar with the A minor pentatonic scale — but just to make sure, here it is in **Example 3**:

Example 3: A Minor Pentatonic Scale

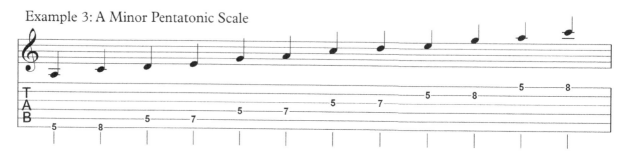

The formula for the minor pentatonic scale is **1-b3-4-5-b7**. In A, we spell it A-C-D-E-G. Remember, *penta* stands for 5, and *tonic* stands for tone—so at its core, a **pentatonic scale** is just a five-tone scale. There are many different pentatonic scales worth investigating!

Practice playing the minor pentatonic scale melodically in fourths, as in **Example 4**:

Example 4: A Minor Pentatonic Scale Melodically in 4ths

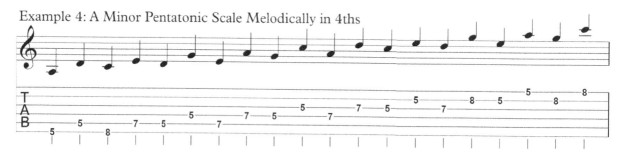

Remember, melodically means we play the notes one after another, as in a melody.

Now practice the minor pentatonic scale in fourths played harmonically, as in **Example 5**:

Example 5: A Minor Pentatonic Played Harmonically in 4ths

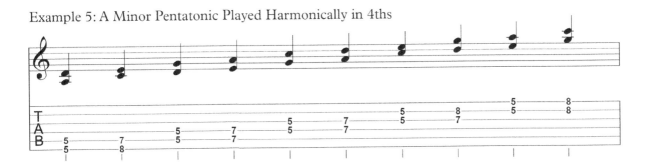

These are both great exercises to practice through all the different forms of the minor pentatonic scale.

Some Voicings

Now let's take the series of fourths we practiced above and transform them into some voicings we can play!

Check out **Example 6** for some quartal voicings from the minor pentatonic scale on the top 3 strings:

Example 6: Quartal Voicings A Minor Pentatonic Top 3 Strings

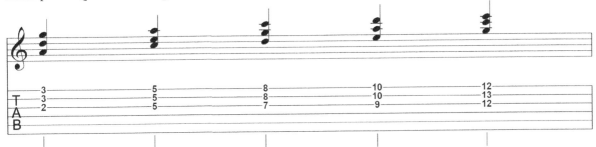

How do these harmonies sound to you? Do they sound clearly defined? Do they sit neatly in place, or do they feel like sand needing to shift around?

Do you recognize some of these shapes as variations on the triads we learned in Level 1? For instance, the second voicing is an A minor triad, and the last voicing is a C major triad.

I know what you're saying: "But those chords aren't built in fourths!" Yes, but when we construct fourths diatonically in the scale, those are the tones that "fit" in that place, even if they aren't truly fourths. Follow me?

Here are the same voicings played on the D, G, and B strings:

Example 7: Quartal Voicings A Minor Pentatonic D, G, B Strings

What do you notice about these voicings? They have the same tones, but the shapes are altered slightly due to the tuning of the guitar. Notice again the A minor triad and C major triad shapes in the scale.

Here are the voicings played an octave lower on the A, D, and G strings:

Example 8: Quartal Voicings A Minor Pentatonic A, D, G Strings

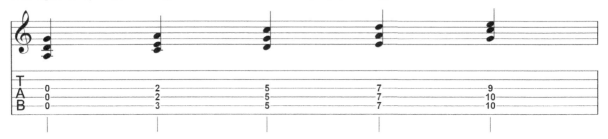

Pretty powerful, huh? These chords have a lot of weight. They're like power chords, but... well, more powerful.

Practice moving these voicings around the fretboard and into different keys outside of A minor. Pick through them, strum them, pluck them with your fingers. Try inverting them and see what happens.

Quartal Harmony in the Major Scale

Now that we've got a feel for quartal harmony in the minor pentatonic scale, let's explore some quartal shapes from the major scale. We will take the same approach.

First, practice playing the major scale melodically in fourths, as in **Example 9**:

Example 9: Diatonic 4ths in C Major Scale Played Melodically

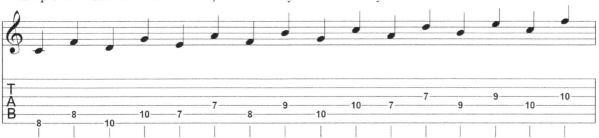

The exercise is written in one octave here, but for the full benefit practice it across two octaves and in all twelve keys.

Next, practice the major scale in fourths melodically:

Example 10: Diatonic 4ths in C Major Scale Played Harmonically

Similarly, practice this exercise in two octaves if you can and in all twelve keys for the most benefit.

Some Quartal Voicings from the Major Scale:

Now let's build a quartal diatonic chord scale from the major scale. See **Example 11** for the details:

Example 11: 4 Note Quartal Harmony in C Major Scale on A, D, G, B String

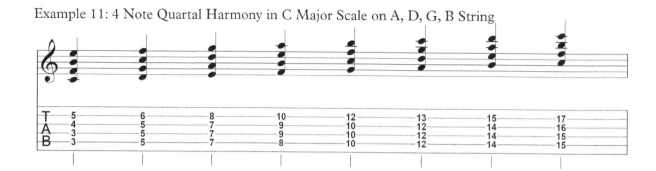

In this example, we have expanded to four-note quartal voicings. Notice the mixture of perfect and augmented fourths in the example.

The first voicing is spelled C-F-B-E. 'C' to 'F' and 'B' to 'E' are both perfect fourths, but 'F' to 'B' is an augmented fourth.

How does this harmony sound to you? What do you feel when you move between this first chord and the second voicing, which is composed entirely of perfect fourths? Can you hear the tensions and resolution there? Can you even resolve to a chord built in perfect fourths? Deep questions that only you can answer for yourself!

How Do We Use These Chords?

Check out **Example 12** below for how you might use these four-note quartal voicings over a D minor vamp.

Example 12: Quartal Voicings Over D Minor Vamp

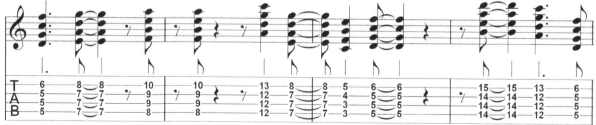

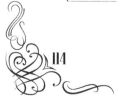

This example is reminiscent of something you might hear from the pianists McCoy Tyner, Bill Evans, or Herbie Hancock. These sort of voicings lend themselves to harmonically open situations like vamps or pedal sections, as they don't point to a specific key center.

Experiment with this concept of moving these voicings in and out of the context of a scale.

Here's an example of quartal harmony being used in a modal context:

Example 13: Quartal Harmony

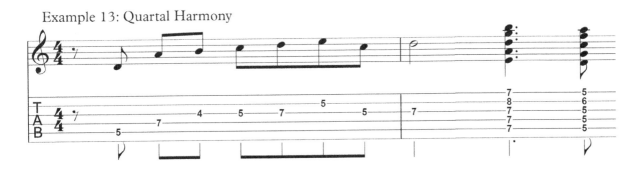

The mode being used here is D dorian — and the two chords at the end of the example are built in fourths from this scale. This is an example of how you can use quartal harmony to "resolve" to a key center.

As I alluded to previously, McCoy Tyner is a pianist who made extensive use of quartal harmony. Here is an example of some of his comping using quartal voicings:

Example 14: Mcoy Tyner Comping

Tyner clearly establishes a key center of F with the heavy fifths (F-C) followed by "**planing**" two quartal harmonies over the bass.

Planing refers to a technique of moving two harmonically ambiguous chords back and forth over a static bass note. This creates a suspended, harmonically open texture.

For something a little older, how about an example of quartal harmony in Claude Debussy's "Sunken Cathedral":

Example 15: Quartal Harmony in Debussy's "Sunken Cathedral"

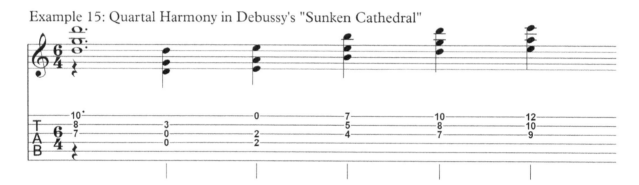

If you've never heard this piece, I highly suggest you find a recording as soon as possible. Like, right now is a good time…

The ascending quartal voicings conjure the image of an enormous cathedral rising out of the mist like something from a science fiction movie. It is a wonderful piece of music.

Here is one more example from Bill Evans:

Example 16: Quartal Harmony in Bill Evan's

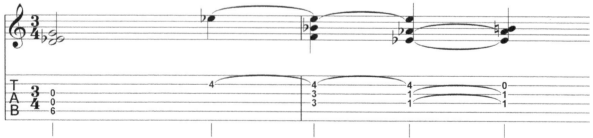

See how in this example he uses "Eb" to connect two quartal voicings? Experiment with this concept. Can you plane parts of a quartal harmony around a common tone? Explore these results.

Here is an example of quartal harmony in rock music:

Example 17: Quartal Harmony in Rock Music

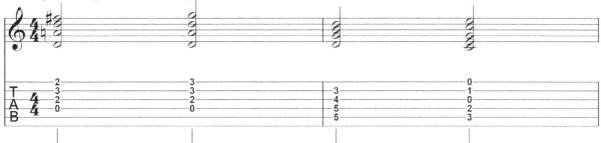

This move from D major to D suspended fourth (sus4) is found in many different songs. But do you see the connection between the second chord in this example and the first quartal voicing in the minor pentatonic scale from Example 6? They're basically the same chord, right? Only the second one has 'D' below it, which leads us to the next idea:

How do we label quartal harmonies over a bass note?

When Things Get Messy: Quartal Harmonies Over Bass Notes

This is an advanced concept. Similar to stacking combinations of triads to build extended and altered dominant chords, we can superimpose quartal voicings over a bass note to create some interesting and fresh harmonies. We use the symbol 'Q' here to denote a quartal harmony.

Check out **Example 18** below

Example 18: GQ/A = A Minor b6, Gsus7/A, Fadd9/A

This harmony presents some ambiguity. What should we call it?

There are a few possibilities. We could call it A minor flat sixth because it has 'C' and 'G', the third and seventh of A minor.

We could call it G suspended seventh over A because it has 'G' (root), 'C' (sus4) , 'F' (seventh) all over 'A'.

We could also call it F add 9 over A because it has 'F' (root), 'A' (third), 'C' (fifth) and 'G' (ninth). This makes the most sense to me. What about you? Any other possibilities you see?

Try this one out:

Example 19: F#Q/A = A Major 6/9

In this example, we have an F# quartal harmony over 'A' in the bass. What should we call this chord? I've labeled it A major 6/9, as that is a common usage for this voicing—but it could also be called B suspended seventh with 'B' as the root, 'E' as the suspended fourth, 'F#' as the fifth, and 'A' as the seventh.

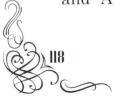

What about this example:

Example 20: CQ/A = Bb Major 9 / A

This is a type of harmony you might find in a pedal 'A' section of music. How would you label this? We have a C quartal chord over 'A' in the bass. I have labeled Bb major ninth over A, but what else could it be?

One more:

Example 21: DQ/A = D Minor 11

This one's a little more straightforward. We have a D quartal voicing over 'A' in the bass. I labeled this chord D minor 11 here because we have 'D' as the root, 'G' as the eleventh, 'A' as the fifth, and 'C' as the seventh.

But you could also label it as a C 6/9 chord, or maybe Eb major seventh sharp eleventh? Rootless? Use your imagination!

Conclusion:

Quartal harmonies are essentially chords stacked in a series of **fourths**. When we build diatonic chord scales in fourths, we have a mixture of perfect and augmented fourths.

We can build quartal harmonies on the guitar from two to six tones, and plane them around the fretboard as we choose to meet the tonal expression we're after.

Quartal harmonies open the gateway to some unique and interesting tensions and resolutions. I hope you take the time to explore these voicings on the guitar and find some ways to incorporate them into your playing and music!

LEVEL 8:
Spread Triads

Intro:

Well, my friend, we have reached the last level on our journey together. We have traveled far as master and pupil, and I hope you have learned a great deal. Before we part ways, there is one last piece of wisdom this old geezer would like to impart on you.

In a sense, we will now return back to where we started. We began this journey together discussing some basics of triads—and so now we will return again to those triads.

This time, we're going to break them apart into what we call **spread triads**.

LEVEL 8 KEYWORDS:

spread triads

What are Spread Triads?

The term spread triads refers to a modification or inversion of the close position triads we learned in Level 1. All we do is take the middle voice and move it up one octave. Not too complicated.

Example 1 below provides a visual detail of this:

Example 1: Close Position Triads Transformed to Spread Triads

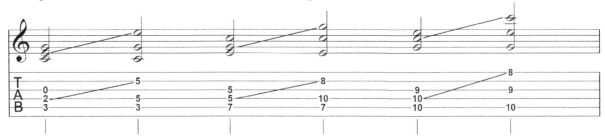

In the first voicing, we move the middle voice 'E' from the root position triad up one octave to form the spread triad. See how this follows in the first and second inversion in this example.

How does this technique change the sound of the chord? I think these spread triads produce a more open and warm sound than the close position triads, which are denser. But what do you think?

Here in **Example 2** are the spread triad inversion on the middle four strings of the guitar:

Example 2: Spread Triads on Middle 4 Strings Two Ways

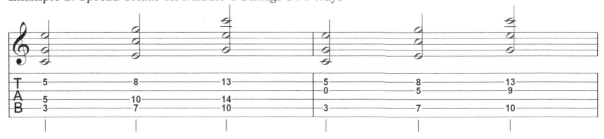

Since there are three notes in a triad, there are two ways to voice them across four strings: The first way uses the A, D, and B string, and the second way uses the A, G, and B strings. Some voicings are easier than others, but it's worth your while to practice and understand both structures.

Check out **Example 3** to see how we voice these spread triads on the top 4 strings:

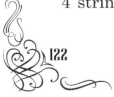

Example 3: Spread Triads on Top 4 Strings Two Ways

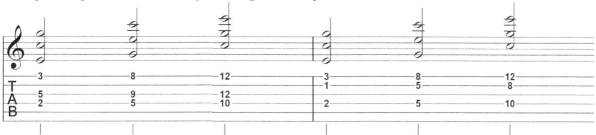

We follow the same steps in this example. First, play through the triads voiced on the D, G, and high E strings, and then play through them on the D, B, and high E strings. Do you see any shapes in common with the shapes from Example 2?

Now, use your music theory knowledge to alter these triads into minor, diminished, and augmented spread triads. Try to use those voicings to build diatonic chord scales with the different inversions we've learned.

Here is an example of how you can use spread triads through a chord progression:

Example 4: Spread Triads in a Cycle of Fourths Progression

Conclusion:

Spread triads are an interesting technique worth exploring to expand your sonic palette beyond the close position inversions we learned early on in Levels 1, 2 and 3. I hope you take the time to explore these sounds! Maybe try to apply some of the triad stacking techniques from Levels 5 and 6 to create some new and interesting harmonies and freshen up your guitar chords!

Conclusion:

What a journey it's been!

Through your meticulous study and disciplined focus, you now possess a much wider scope of knowledge and of guitar chords. So many new opportunities are now open to you! Which path will you follow?

Will you continue to develop your **triads**? Can you expand beyond the four triad qualities we learned here to include all sets of three notes? What about a triad spelled C-D-F? Or C-A-B? How would you incorporate shapes like that into your guitar style?

Can you break out of the **CAGED system** and identify discreet triad shapes inside the CAGED chords? What if you alter the tuning of the guitar? Would the CAGED system still be valid, or does another system emerge?

Where will you go with **symmetrical chords**? The nature of the guitar fretboard lends itself to intuitive symmetrical patterns. Explore this to realms outside of traditional music theory.

What about **seventh chords**, **alterations**, and **extensions**? There is a whole universe inside these chords you could spend lifetimes exploring. Dive in and enjoy!

What about chords with two or three alterations? Dominant seventh sharp ninth, sharp eleventh?

And what about **quartal harmony**? After all, standard guitar tuning is built in fourths — perfect for quartal harmony. What about inversions of the quartal shapes we learned in Level 7? What kind of fresh, cosmic colors can you generate with these harmonies?

No matter what road you take, one thing's for sure: the guitar is a complex, infinite matrix. It's an ever-evolving system of interlocking patterns and shapes—and it is your duty as a guitarist to explore and eventually come to an understanding of these mysteries!

Hopefully *the Chords Bible* has been of assistance to you on your journey and you continue to revisit these pages as you progress!

Until then, good luck my friend!

Farewell!

Pssssttt....

What are you doing here? Are you lost?

Do people even look at the last pages of a book?

Jokes aside, I hope you enjoyed this book. I certainly loved the process of writing it.

If you enjoyed this book, could you take 2 minutes to leave a review about it?

Reviews are the lifeblood for small publishers and help us get our books into the hands of more guitarists like you.

We read every review personally and appreciate each one of it.

To leave a review, simply go to the platform you purchased the book from and type in your review.

With that said, here's Guitar Head signing off!

Until next time then? I'll see you in another book.

Chord dictionary

A Maj | A Major

Spelling: 1, 3, 5

A Maj7 | A Major 7

Spelling: 1, 3, 5, 7

A Maj9 | A Major 9

Spelling: 1, 3, 5, 7, 9

A Maj11 | A Major 11

Spelling: 1, 3, 5, 7, 9, 11

129

A Maj13	A Major 13

Spelling: 1, 3, 5, 7, 9, 11, 13

A Min	A Minor

Spelling: 1, b3, 5

A Min7	A Minor 7

Spelling: 1, b3, 5, b7

A Min9	A Minor 9

Spelling: 1, b3, 5, b7, 9

A Min11 | A Minor 11

Spelling: 1, b3, 5, b7, 9, 11

A Min13 | A Minor 13

Spelling: 1, b3, 5, b7, 9, 11, 13

A7 | A Dominant 7

Spelling: 1, 3, 5, b7

A9 | A Dominant 9

Spelling: 1, 3, 5, b7, 9

A11	A Dominant 11

Spelling: 1, 3, 5, b7, 9, 11

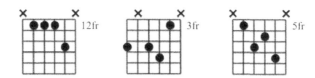

A13	A Dominant 13

Spelling: 1, 3, 5, b7, 9, 11, 13

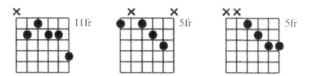

A7b9	A Dominant 7 Flat 9

Spelling: 1, 3, 5, b7, b9

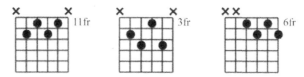

A7#9	A Dominant 7 Sharp 9

Spelling: 1, 3, 5, b7, #9

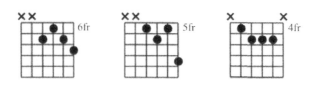

A7#11

A Dominant 7 Sharp 11

Spelling: 1, 3, 5, b7, 9, #11

A7b13

A Dominant 7 Flat 13

Spelling: 1, 3, 5, b7, 9, 11, b13

A7sus4

A Dominant 7 Suspended 4

Spelling: 1, 4, 5, b7

AMin7b5

A Minor 7 Flat 5

Spelling: 1, b3, b5, b7

133

A Dim7, A°7	A Diminished 7

Spelling: 1, b3, b5, bb7

A Aug, A⁺	A Augmented

Spelling: 1, 3, #5

AQ	A Quartal

Spelling: 1, 4, b7

A#/Bb Maj	A#/Bb Major

Spelling: 1, 3, 5

A#/Bb Maj7	A#/Bb Major 7

Spelling: 1, 3, 5, 7

A#/Bb Maj9	A#/Bb Major 9

Spelling: 1, 3, 5, 7, 9

A#/Bb Maj11	A#/Bb Major 11

Spelling: 1, 3, 5, 7, 9, 11

135

A#/Bb Maj13 | A#/Bb Major 13

Spelling: 1, 3, 5, 7, 9, 11, 13

A#/Bb Min | A#/Bb Minor

Spelling: 1, b3, 5

A#/Bb Min7 | A#/Bb Minor 7

Spelling: 1, b3, 5, b7

A#/Bb Min9 | A#/Bb Minor 9

Spelling: 1, b3, 5, b7, 9

A#/Bb Min11 | A#/Bb Minor 11

Spelling: 1, b3, 5, b7, 9, 11

A#/Bb Min13 | A#/Bb Minor 13

Spelling: 1, b3, 5, b7, 9, 11, 13

A#/Bb7 | A#/Bb Dominant 7

Spelling: 1, 3, 5, b7

A#/Bb9 | A#/Bb Dominant 9

Spelling: 1, 3, 5, b7, 9

A#/Bb11 | A#/Bb Dominant 11

Spelling: 1, 3, 5, b7, 9, 11

A#/Bb13 | A#/Bb Dominant 13

Spelling: 1, 3, 5, b7, 9, 11, 13

A#/Bb7b9 | A#/Bb Dominant 7 Flat 9

Spelling: 1, 3, 5, b7, b9

A#/Bb7#9 | A#/Bb Dominant 7 Sharp 9

Spelling: 1, 3, 5, b7, #9

| A#/Bb7#11 | A#/Bb Dominant 7 Sharp 11 |

Spelling: 1, 3, 5, b7, 9, #11

| A#/Bb7b13 | A#/Bb Dominant 7 Flat 13 |

Spelling: 1, 3, 5, b7, 9, 11, b13

| A#/Bb7sus4 | A#/Bb Dominant 7 Suspended 4 |

Spelling: 1, 4, 5, b7

| A#/BbMin7b5 | A#/Bb Minor 7 Flat 5 |

Spelling: 1, b3, b5, b7

139

A#/Bb Dim7, A#/Bb °7 | A#/Bb Diminished 7

Spelling: 1, b3, b5, bb7

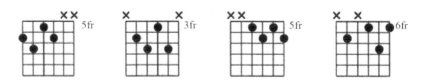

A#/Bb Aug, A#/Bb⁺ | A#/Bb Augmented

Spelling: 1, 3, #5

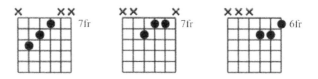

A#/BbQ | A#/Bb Quartal

Spelling: 1, 4, b7

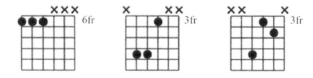

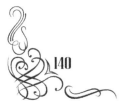

B Maj | B Major

Spelling: 1, 3, 5

B Maj7 | B Major 7

Spelling: 1, 3, 5, 7

B Maj9 | B Major 9

Spelling: 1, 3, 5, 7, 9

B Maj11 | B Major 11

Spelling: 1, 3, 5, 7, 9, 11

B Maj13 | B Major 13

Spelling: 1, 3, 5, 7, 9, 11, 13

B Min | B Minor

Spelling: 1, b3, 5

B Min7 | B Minor 7

Spelling: 1, b3, 5, b7

B Min9 | B Minor 9

Spelling: 1, b3, 5, b7, 9

  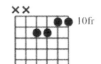

B Min11 | B Minor 11

Spelling: 1, b3, 5, b7, 9, 11

B Min13 | B Minor 13

Spelling: 1, b3, 5, b7, 9, 11, 13

B7 | B Dominant 7

Spelling: 1, 3, 5, b7

B9 | B Dominant 9

Spelling: 1, 3, 5, b7, 9

B11	B Dominant 11

Spelling: 1, 3, 5, b7, 9, 11

B13	B Dominant 13

Spelling: 1, 3, 5, b7, 9, 11, 13

B7b9	B Dominant 7 Flat 9

Spelling: 1, 3, 5, b7, b9

B7#9	B Dominant 7 Sharp 9

Spelling: 1, 3, 5, b7, #9

144

B7#11

B Dominant 7 Sharp 11

Spelling: 1, 3, 5, b7, 9, #11

B7b13

B Dominant 7 Flat 13

Spelling: 1, 3, 5, b7, 9, 11, b13

B7sus4

B Dominant 7 Suspended 4

Spelling: 1, 4, 5, b7

BMin7b5

B Minor 7 Flat 5

Spelling: 1, b3, b5, b7

| B Dim7, B°7 | B Diminished 7 |

Spelling: 1, b3, b5, bb7

| B Aug, B⁺ | B Augmented |

Spelling: 1, 3, #5

| BQ | B Quartal |

Spelling: 1, 4, b7

C Maj | C Major

Spelling: 1, 3, 5

C Maj7 | C Major 7

Spelling: 1, 3, 5, 7

C Maj9 | C Major 9

Spelling: 1, 3, 5, 7, 9

C Maj11 | C Major 11

Spelling: 1, 3, 5, 7, 9, 11

C Maj13	C Major 13

Spelling: 1, 3, 5, 7, 9, 11, 13

C Min	C Minor

Spelling: 1, b3, 5

C Min7	C Minor 7

Spelling: 1, b3, 5, b7

C Min9	C Minor 9

Spelling: 1, b3, 5, b7, 9

  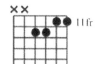

C Min11 | C Minor 11

Spelling: 1, b3, 5, b7, 9, 11

C Min13 | C Minor 13

Spelling: 1, b3, 5, b7, 9, 11, 13

C7 | C Dominant 7

Spelling: 1, 3, 5, b7

C9 | C Dominant 9

Spelling: 1, 3, 5, b7, 9

149

C11	C Dominant 11

Spelling: 1, 3, 5, b7, 9, 11

C13	C Dominant 13

Spelling: 1, 3, 5, b7, 9, 11, 13

C7b9	C Dominant 7 Flat 9

Spelling: 1, 3, 5, b7, b9

C7#9	C Dominant 7 Sharp 9

Spelling: 1, 3, 5, b7, #9

C7#11 | C Dominant 7 Sharp 11

Spelling: 1, 3, 5, b7, 9, #11

C7b13 | C Dominant 7 Flat 13

Spelling: 1, 3, 5, b7, 9, 11, b13

C7sus4 | C Dominant 7 Suspended 4

Spelling: 1, 4, 5, b7

CMin7b5 | C Minor 7 Flat 5

Spelling: 1, b3, b5, b7

C Dim7, C°7	C Diminished 7

Spelling: 1, b3, b5, bb7

C Aug, C⁺	C Augmented

Spelling: 1, 3, #5

CQ	C Quartal

Spelling: 1, 4, b7

C#/Db Maj	C#/Db Major

Spelling: 1, 3, 5

C#/Db Maj7	C#/Db Major 7

Spelling: 1, 3, 5, 7

C#/Db Maj9	C#/Db Major 9

Spelling: 1, 3, 5, 7, 9

C#/Db Maj11	C#/Db Major 11

Spelling: 1, 3, 5, 7, 9, 11

153

C#/Db Maj13	C#/Db Major 13

Spelling: 1, 3, 5, 7, 9, 11, 13

C#/Db Min	C#/Db Minor

Spelling: 1, b3, 5

C#/Db Min7	C#/Db Minor 7

Spelling: 1, b3, 5, b7

C#/Db Min9	C#/Db Minor 9

Spelling: 1, b3, 5, b7, 9

C#/Db Min11 | C#/Db Minor 11

Spelling: 1, b3, 5, b7, 9, 11

C#/Db Min13 | C#/Db Minor 13

Spelling: 1, b3, 5, b7, 9, 11, 13

C#/Db7 | C#/Db Dominant 7

Spelling: 1, 3, 5, b7

C#/Db9 | C#/Db Dominant 9

Spelling: 1, 3, 5, b7, 9

C#/Db11	C#/Db Dominant 11

Spelling: 1, 3, 5, b7, 9, 11

C#/Db13	C#/Db Dominant 13

Spelling: 1, 3, 5, b7, 9, 11, 13

C#/Db7b9	C#/Db Dominant 7 Flat 9

Spelling: 1, 3, 5, b7, b9

C#/Db7#9	C#/Db Dominant 7 Sharp 9

Spelling: 1, 3, 5, b7, #9

C#/Db7#11	C#/Db Dominant 7 Sharp 11

Spelling: 1, 3, 5, b7, 9, #11

C#/Db7b13	C#/Db Dominant 7 Flat 13

Spelling: 1, 3, 5, b7, 9, 11, b13

C#/Db7sus4	C#/Db Dominant 7 Suspended 4

Spelling: 1, 4, 5, b7

C#/DbMin7b5	C#/Db Minor 7 Flat 5

Spelling: 1, b3, b5, b7

C#/Db Dim7, C#/Db°7 | C#/Db Diminished 7

Spelling: 1, b3, b5, bb7

C#/Db Aug, C#/Db⁺ | C#/Db Augmented

Spelling: 1, 3, #5

C#/DbQ | C#/Db Quartal

Spelling: 1, 4, b7

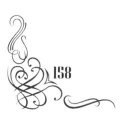

D Maj | D Major

Spelling: 1, 3, 5

D Maj7 | D Major 7

Spelling: 1, 3, 5, 7

D Maj9 | D Major 9

Spelling: 1, 3, 5, 7, 9

D Maj11 | D Major 11

Spelling: 1, 3, 5, 7, 9, 11

159

D Maj13 | D Major 13

Spelling: 1, 3, 5, 7, 9, 11, 13

D Min | D Minor

Spelling: 1, b3, 5

D Min7 | D Minor 7

Spelling: 1, b3, 5, b7

D Min9 | D Minor 9

Spelling: 1, b3, 5, b7, 9

D Min11	D Minor 11

Spelling: 1, b3, 5, b7, 9, 11

D Min13	D Minor 13

Spelling: 1, b3, 5, b7, 9, 11, 13

D7	D Dominant 7

Spelling: 1, 3, 5, b7

D9	D Dominant 9

Spelling: 1, 3, 5, b7, 9

D11 | D Dominant 11

Spelling: 1, 3, 5, b7, 9, 11

D13 | D Dominant 13

Spelling: 1, 3, 5, b7, 9, 11, 13

D7b9 | D Dominant 7 Flat 9

Spelling: 1, 3, 5, b7, b9

D7#9 | D Dominant 7 Sharp 9

Spelling: 1, 3, 5, b7, #9

D7#11 | D Dominant 7 Sharp 11

Spelling: 1, 3, 5, b7, 9, #11

D7b13 | D Dominant 7 Flat 13

Spelling: 1, 3, 5, b7, 9, 11, b13

D7sus4 | D Dominant 7 Suspended 4

Spelling: 1, 4, 5, b7

DMin7b5 | D Minor 7 Flat 5

Spelling: 1, b3, b5, b7

D Dim7, D°7	D Diminished 7

Spelling: 1, b3, b5, bb7

D Aug, D⁺	D Augmented

Spelling: 1, 3, #5

DQ	D Quartal

Spelling: 1, 4, b7

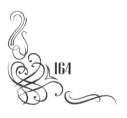

D#/Eb Maj | D#/Eb Major

Spelling: 1, 3, 5

D#/Eb Maj7 | D#/Eb Major 7

Spelling: 1, 3, 5, 7

D#/Eb Maj9 | D#/Eb Major 9

Spelling: 1, 3, 5, 7, 9

D#/Eb Maj11 | D#/Eb Major 11

Spelling: 1, 3, 5, 7, 9, 11

D#/Eb Maj13 | D#/Eb Major 13

Spelling: 1, 3, 5, 7, 9, 11, 13

D#/Eb Min | D#/Eb Minor

Spelling: 1, b3, 5

D#/Eb Min7 | D#/Eb Minor 7

Spelling: 1, b3, 5, b7

D#/Eb Min9 | D#/Eb Minor 9

Spelling: 1, b3, 5, b7, 9

D#/Eb Min11 | D#/Eb Minor 11

Spelling: 1, b3, 5, b7, 9, 11

D#/Eb Min13 | D#/Eb Minor 13

Spelling: 1, b3, 5, b7, 9, 11, 13

D#/Eb7 | D#/Eb Dominant 7

Spelling: 1, 3, 5, b7

D#/Eb9 | D#/Eb Dominant 9

Spelling: 1, 3, 5, b7, 9

D#/Eb11 | D#/Eb Dominant 11

Spelling: 1, 3, 5, b7, 9, 11

D#/Eb13 | D#/Eb Dominant 13

Spelling: 1, 3, 5, b7, 9, 11, 13

D#/Eb7b9 | D#/Eb Dominant 7 Flat 9

Spelling: 1, 3, 5, b7, b9

D#/Eb7#9 | D#/Eb Dominant 7 Sharp 9

Spelling: 1, 3, 5, b7, #9

D#/Eb7#11	D#/Eb Dominant 7 Sharp 11

Spelling: 1, 3, 5, b7, 9, #11

D#/Eb7b13	D#/Eb Dominant 7 Flat 13

Spelling: 1, 3, 5, b7, 9, 11, b13

D#/Eb7sus4	D#/Eb Dominant 7 Suspended 4

Spelling: 1, 4, 5, b7

D#/EbMin7b5	D#/Eb Minor 7 Flat 5

Spelling: 1, b3, b5, b7

D#/Eb Dim7, D#/Eb°7 | D#/Eb Diminished 7

Spelling: 1, b3, b5, bb7

D#/Eb Aug, D#/Eb⁺ | D#/Eb Augmented

Spelling: 1, 3, #5

D#/EbQ | D#/Eb Quartal

Spelling: 1, 4, b7

170

E Maj	E Major

Spelling: 1, 3, 5

E Maj7	E Major 7

Spelling: 1, 3, 5, 7

E Maj9	E Major 9

Spelling: 1, 3, 5, 7, 9

E Maj11	E Major 11

Spelling: 1, 3, 5, 7, 9, 11

171

E Maj13 | E Major 13

Spelling: 1, 3, 5, 7, 9, 11, 13

E Min | E Minor

Spelling: 1, b3, 5

E Min7 | E Minor 7

Spelling: 1, b3, 5, b7

E Min9 | E Minor 9

Spelling: 1, b3, 5, b7, 9

E Min11 | E Minor 11

Spelling: 1, b3, 5, b7, 9, 11

E Min13 | E Minor 13

Spelling: 1, b3, 5, b7, 9, 11, 13

E7 | E Dominant 7

Spelling: 1, 3, 5, b7

E9 | E Dominant 9

Spelling: 1, 3, 5, b7, 9

E11 | E Dominant 11

Spelling: 1, 3, 5, b7, 9, 11

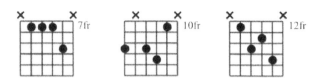

E13 | E Dominant 13

Spelling: 1, 3, 5, b7, 9, 11, 13

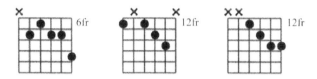

E7b9 | E Dominant 7 Flat 9

Spelling: 1, 3, 5, b7, b9

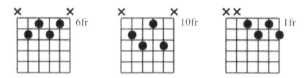

E7#9 | E Dominant 7 Sharp 9

Spelling: 1, 3, 5, b7, #9

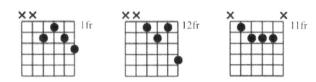

E7#11 | E Dominant 7 Sharp 11

Spelling: 1, 3, 5, b7, 9, #11

E7b13 | E Dominant 7 Flat 13

Spelling: 1, 3, 5, b7, 9, 11, b13

E7sus4 | E Dominant 7 Suspended 4

Spelling: 1, 4, 5, b7

EMin7b5 | E Minor 7 Flat 5

Spelling: 1, b3, b5, b7

E Dim7, E°7	E Diminished 7

Spelling: 1, b3, b5, bb7

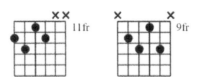 

E Aug, E⁺	E Augmented

Spelling: 1, 3, #5

EQ	E Quartal

Spelling: 1, 4, b7

F Maj | F Major

Spelling: 1, 3, 5

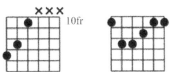

F Maj7 | F Major 7

Spelling: 1, 3, 5, 7

F Maj9 | F Major 9

Spelling: 1, 3, 5, 7, 9

F Maj11 | F Major 11

Spelling: 1, 3, 5, 7, 9, 11

F Maj13	F Major 13

Spelling: 1, 3, 5, 7, 9, 11, 13

F Min	F Minor

Spelling: 1, b3, 5

F Min7	F Minor 7

Spelling: 1, b3, 5, b7

F Min9	F Minor 9

Spelling: 1, b3, 5, b7, 9

F Min11 | F Minor 11

Spelling: 1, b3, 5, b7, 9, 11

F Min13 | F Minor 13

Spelling: 1, b3, 5, b7, 9, 11, 13

F7 | F Dominant 7

Spelling: 1, 3, 5, b7

F9 | F Dominant 9

Spelling: 1, 3, 5, b7, 9

F11 | F Dominant 11

Spelling: 1, 3, 5, b7, 9, 11

F13 | F Dominant 13

Spelling: 1, 3, 5, b7, 9, 11, 13

F7b9 | F Dominant 7 Flat 9

Spelling: 1, 3, 5, b7, b9

F7#9 | F Dominant 7 Sharp 9

Spelling: 1, 3, 5, b7, #9

F7#11 | F Dominant 7 Sharp 11

Spelling: 1, 3, 5, b7, 9, #11

F7b13 | F Dominant 7 Flat 13

Spelling: 1, 3, 5, b7, 9, 11, b13

F7sus4 | F Dominant 7 Suspended 4

Spelling: 1, 4, 5, b7

FMin7b5 | F Minor 7 Flat 5

Spelling: 1, b3, b5, b7

F Dim7, F°7 | F Diminished 7

Spelling: 1, b3, b5, bb7

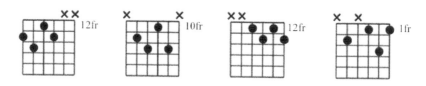

F Aug, F⁺ | F Augmented

Spelling: 1, 3, #5

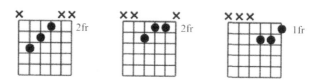

FQ | F Quartal

Spelling: 1, 4, b7

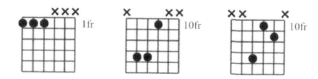

F#/Gb Maj | F#/Gb Major

Spelling: 1, 3, 5

F#/Gb Maj7 | F#/Gb Major 7

Spelling: 1, 3, 5, 7

F#/Gb Maj9 | F#/Gb Major 9

Spelling: 1, 3, 5, 7, 9

F#/Gb Maj11 | F#/Gb Major 11

Spelling: 1, 3, 5, 7, 9, 11

F#/Gb Maj13 | F#/Gb Major 13

Spelling: 1, 3, 5, 7, 9, 11, 13

F#/Gb Min | F#/Gb Minor

Spelling: 1, b3, 5

F#/Gb Min7 | F#/Gb Minor 7

Spelling: 1, b3, 5, b7

F#/Gb Min9 | F#/Gb Minor 9

Spelling: 1, b3, 5, b7, 9

F#/Gb Min11 | **F#/Gb Minor 11**

Spelling: 1, b3, 5, b7, 9, 11

F#/Gb Min13 | **F#/Gb Minor 13**

Spelling: 1, b3, 5, b7, 9, 11, 13

F#/Gb7 | **F#/Gb Dominant 7**

Spelling: 1, 3, 5, b7

F#/Gb9 | **F#/Gb Dominant 9**

Spelling: 1, 3, 5, b7, 9

F#/Gb11 | F#/Gb Dominant 11

Spelling: 1, 3, 5, b7, 9, 11

F#/Gb13 | F#/Gb Dominant 13

Spelling: 1, 3, 5, b7, 9, 11, 13

F#/Gb7b9 | F#/Gb Dominant 7 Flat 9

Spelling: 1, 3, 5, b7, b9

F#/Gb7#9 | F#/Gb Dominant 7 Sharp 9

Spelling: 1, 3, 5, b7, #9

F#/Gb7#11	F#/Gb Dominant 7 Sharp 11

Spelling: 1, 3, 5, b7, 9, #11

F#/Gb7b13	F#/Gb Dominant 7 Flat 13

Spelling: 1, 3, 5, b7, 9, 11, b13

F#/Gb7sus4	F#/Gb Dominant 7 Suspended 4

Spelling: 1, 4, 5, b7

F#/GbMin7b5	F#/Gb Minor 7 Flat 5

Spelling: 1, b3, b5, b7

F#/Gb Dim7, F#/Gb°7 | F#/Gb Diminished 7

Spelling: 1, b3, b5, bb7

F#/Gb Aug, F#/Gb⁺ | F#/Gb Augmented

Spelling: 1, 3, #5

F#/GbQ | F#/Gb Quartal

Spelling: 1, 4, b7

| **G Maj** | **G Major** |

Spelling: 1, 3, 5

| **G Maj7** | **G Major 7** |

Spelling: 1, 3, 5, 7

| **G Maj9** | **G Major 9** |

Spelling: 1, 3, 5, 7, 9

| **G Maj11** | **G Major 11** |

Spelling: 1, 3, 5, 7, 9, 11

G Maj13	G Major 13

Spelling: 1, 3, 5, 7, 9, 11, 13

G Min	G Minor

Spelling: 1, b3, 5

G Min7	G Minor 7

Spelling: 1, b3, 5, b7

G Min9	G Minor 9

Spelling: 1, b3, 5, b7, 9

G Min11 | G Minor 11

Spelling: 1, b3, 5, b7, 9, 11

G Min13 | G Minor 13

Spelling: 1, b3, 5, b7, 9, 11, 13

G7 | G Dominant 7

Spelling: 1, 3, 5, b7

G9 | G Dominant 9

Spelling: 1, 3, 5, b7, 9

G11 | G Dominant 11

Spelling: 1, 3, 5, b7, 9, 11

G13 | G Dominant 13

Spelling: 1, 3, 5, b7, 9, 11, 13

G7b9 | G Dominant 7 Flat 9

Spelling: 1, 3, 5, b7, b9

G7#9 | G Dominant 7 Sharp 9

Spelling: 1, 3, 5, b7, #9

G7#11 | G Dominant 7 Sharp 11

Spelling: 1, 3, 5, b7, 9, #11

G7b13 | G Dominant 7 Flat 13

Spelling: 1, 3, 5, b7, 9, 11, b13

G7sus4 | G Dominant 7 Suspended 4

Spelling: 1, 4, 5, b7

GMin7b5 | G Minor 7 Flat 5

Spelling: 1, b3, b5, b7

G Dim7, G°7 | G Diminished 7

Spelling: 1, b3, b5, bb7

G Aug, G⁺ | G Augmented

Spelling: 1, 3, #5

GQ | G Quartal

Spelling: 1, 4, b7

G#/Ab Maj | **G#/Ab Major**

Spelling: 1, 3, 5

G#/Ab Maj7 | **G#/Ab Major 7**

Spelling: 1, 3, 5, 7

G#/Ab Maj9 | **G#/Ab Major 9**

Spelling: 1, 3, 5, 7, 9

G#/Ab Maj11 | **G#/Ab Major 11**

Spelling: 1, 3, 5, 7, 9, 11

G#/Ab Maj13 | G#/Ab Major 13

Spelling: 1, 3, 5, 7, 9, 11, 13

G#/Ab Min | G#/Ab Minor

Spelling: 1, b3, 5

G#/Ab Min7 | G#/Ab Minor 7

Spelling: 1, b3, 5, b7

G#/Ab Min9 | G#/Ab Minor 9

Spelling: 1, b3, 5, b7, 9

G#/Ab Min11 | G#/Ab Minor 11

Spelling: 1, b3, 5, b7, 9, 11

G#/Ab Min13 | G#/Ab Minor 13

Spelling: 1, b3, 5, b7, 9, 11, 13

G#/Ab7 | G#/Ab Dominant 7

Spelling: 1, 3, 5, b7

G#/Ab9 | G#/Ab Dominant 9

Spelling: 1, 3, 5, b7, 9

197

G#/Ab11 | G#/Ab Dominant 11

Spelling: 1, 3, 5, b7, 9, 11

G#/Ab13 | G#/Ab Dominant 13

Spelling: 1, 3, 5, b7, 9, 11, 13

G#/Ab7b9 | G#/Ab Dominant 7 Flat 9

Spelling: 1, 3, 5, b7, b9

G#/Ab7#9 | G#/Ab Dominant 7 Sharp 9

Spelling: 1, 3, 5, b7, #9

G#/Ab7#11

| G#/Ab Dominant 7 |
| Sharp 11 |

Spelling: 1, 3, 5, b7, 9, #11

G#/Ab7b13

| G#/Ab Dominant 7 |
| Flat 13 |

Spelling: 1, 3, 5, b7, 9, 11, b13

G#/Ab7sus4

| G#/Ab Dominant 7 |
| Suspended 4 |

Spelling: 1, 4, 5, b7

G#/AbMin7b5

| G#/Ab Minor 7 Flat 5 |

Spelling: 1, b3, b5, b7

G#/Ab Dim7, G#/Ab°7 | G#/Ab Diminished 7

Spelling: 1, b3, b5, bb7

G#/Ab Aug, G#/Ab⁺ | G#/Ab Augmented

Spelling: 1, 3, #5

G#/AbQ | G#/Ab Quartal

Spelling: 1, 4, b7

THE END

Guitar Notation

Ok, before you get overwhelmed by the weird diagrams below, let me explain.

Guitar Tablature has more to it than just strings and fret numbers. You might have come across some strange signs and symbols while learning your lick or exercises. We call them Notation Legends.

Here we have listed some of them you often bump into.

HAMMER-ON:
Pick the lower note first, then hit the second note with a finger of left hand without picking.

PULL-OFF:
Pick the higher note first, then pull the finger off to sound the second note. Make sure both fingers are placed at the same time before the first hit

PTHRILL:
Pick the first note and alternate rapidly between that note and the one in brackets using hammer-ons and pull-offs.

LEGATO SLIDE:
Pick the first note and, using the same finger, slide through the fretboard until next note. Don't struck the next note

TAPPING: With a finger of the pick hand hammer-on the note indicated with + sign (T on the tab) and then pull-off to the lower note fretted by the fret hand.

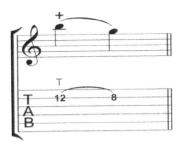

WHOLE-STEP BEND:
Pick the note and then bend up a whole tone.

SLIDE:
Pick the first note and, using the same finger, slide through the fretboard until next note. The next

PALM MUTING:
Place the side of the palm of the pick hand right before the bridge to touch lightly the string(s) and produce a muted sound.

HALF-STEP BEND:
Pick the note and then bend up a half tone.

VIBRATO: With the fretting hand vibrate the string up and down using small bends and releases. Exaggerate the effect to create a wide vibrato.

MUFFLED STRINGS:
Place the fret hand across the strings with a slightly touch (without pressing the strings against the fret), strum with the pick hand to produce a percussive sound.

QUARTER-TONE BEND:
Pick the note and then bend up a quarter-tone

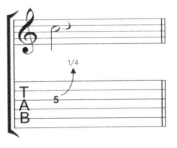

BEND AND RELEASE:
Pick the note, bend the amount indicated and then release the bend to the first note.

GRACE NOTE BEND:
Pick the note, and bend the amount indicated immediately.

PRE-BEND:
First bend the string the amount indicated and then strike the string.

PRE-BEND & RELEASE:
First bend the string the amount indicated, strike the string and then release the bend.

NATURAL HARMONIC:
Play the note placing the fret hand finger lightly over the string directly at the fret indicated and releasing the finger after the note starts to ring.

WHAMMY BAR SCOOP:
Press down the bar just before striking the note and then release the push returning the bar to original place.

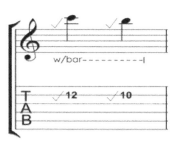

PINCH HARMONIC:
Place the fret hand finger normally and with the pick hand, strike the note normally and at the same time the edge of the thumb has to make contact with the string.

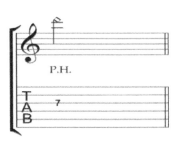

ARTIFICIAL HARMONIC:
Fret the note normally, then lightly place your index finger directly over the fret indicated in parenthesis, then pick the note with your thumb or ring finger.

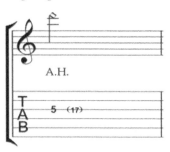

WHAMMY BAR DIVE AND RETURN: Play the note, then, push down the bar to produce the pitch indicated with the number and finally release the push returning bar to original place.

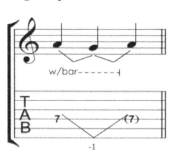

60566699R00117